Praise for *Optimizing the Power of Action Learning*

"There is a Chinese proverb—'We learn when we are engaged in action.'
This book shows how to optimize this proverb!"
> Florence Ho Hau Ching, Director, Human Resources,
> Sun Hung Kai Financial Group

"Action learning is extremely powerful in taking advantage of diversity
within teams—a way for organizations to deal with complexity. This book
outlines how this works in today's organizations."
> Pascal Etzol, Director, IS Finance, Aventis

"Relevant to organizations, be they corporate, private, or nonprofit, and
demonstrates clearly the steps needed to turn a powerful concept into
practical and beneficial action."
> Clive Watkins, Principal Management Development Consultant,
> The Management Centre, London

"Provides managers and leaders with the key ingredients to transform their
people into lifelong learners."
> Dr. Mohd Effendy Rajab, Director, Adult Resources, World Scout Bureau

"Action learning is a simple but powerful technique that helps to accomplish
results in our complex business environment."
> Rubens Pessanha, CEO, Alumni of Coppead/Brazil

"Brilliant! Marquardt has helped guide us to use action learning to develop
our leadership competencies, align with our corporate values, and solve our
most difficult problems."
> Harry Lenderman, Ed.D., Revans Professor, International Management
> Centres Association; Academic Dean, Sodexho University

"If you care about organizational learning, if you care about individual
learning, don't dare plan a training or education initiative in your organization without first drawing on Marquardt's 30 years of experience in action
learning!"
> Robert Kramer, Ph.D., Director, AU/OPM and Key Executive
> Education Programs, American University

"It's not just the breadth of Marquardt's experience in corporations, government agencies, and nonprofit organizations—it's the everyday practicality of
his ideas that can be put to use in the workplace."
> Howard Schuman, Human Resources Advisor, Central Bank of Sri Lanka

"The strength of action learning lies in its ability to transform group dialogue
from 'talk to' to 'talk with,' and group actions from 'talk about' to 'next
steps.'"
> Colleen E. Duffy, Principal Consultant, Lafferty Associates

"This book further develops the concepts and ensures successful applications of action learning."

Dr. Antony Hii, Regional Dean for Asia,
International Management Centres Association

"The case studies in this book resonate with the results I have experienced and demonstrate the effectiveness of Marquardt's approach."

Deborah Waddill, Restek Consulting

"By far the best book I have read on the subject of action learning. I say that for three reasons: the content is rich, the examples are illustrative of the content, and it reads well."

Joanne J. Jorz, Director of Business and Product Development,
The Odyssey Group

"Exactly what is needed in successful organizations in order to compete in the global market."

Pentti Sydanmaanlakka, Ph.D., Managing Director,
Pertec Consulting Ltd.; author of An Intelligent Organization

"Provides a framework, specific tools, and real examples of how organizations have implemented action learning to increase performance. Anyone leading teams of people who wants to capture and disseminate their learnings will find direct application for the knowledge Marquardt is sharing."

Carol Gorelick, Ed.D., Principal, Solutions for Information
& Management Services, Inc.; coauthor of Performance Through Learning

"A must read for anyone who wants to improve the effectiveness of people and organizations."

Doug Bryant, Vice President, Organizational Development and Training,
Advance Auto Parts

"A very valuable tool for fully understanding the rationale behind action learning and the astonishing benefits that can be obtained from its application."

Faccio Marisa, CEO, Accademia srl

"Serves as a compass to guide organizations on their journey to achieve the benefits of action learning. This brilliant book will become an action learning classic."

Taebok Lee, President, Paradigm Consulting Associates;
author of Change: Here to Stay

"A great 'how-to' book. A quick and easy reference guide. Makes clear the roles and responsibilities of each of the action learning participants. Guides the reader through the process of forming a powerful action learning team. The advice for the action learning coach is invaluable."

Bernadette Carson, President, BKE Corporation

Optimizing the Power of Action Learning

Solving Problems and Building Leaders in Real Time

Michael J. Marquardt

 DAVIES-BLACK PUBLISHING
Mountain View, California

Published by Davies-Black Publishing, a division of CPP, Inc., 1055 Joaquin Road, Suite 200, Mountain View, CA 94043; 800-624-1765.

Special discounts on bulk quantities of Davies-Black books are available to corporations, professional associations, and other organizations. For details, contact the Director of Marketing and Sales at Davies-Black Publishing; 650-691-9123; fax 650-623-9271.

Visit the Davies-Black Publishing Web site at www.daviesblack.com.

08 07 06 05 04   10 9 8 7 6 5 4 3
Printed in the United States of America

Library of Congress Cataloging-in-Publication Data
Marquardt, Michael J.
 Optimizing the power of action learning : solving problems and building leaders in real time / Michael J. Marquardt.—1st ed.
  p. cm.
Includes biographical references.
 ISBN 0-89106-191-6
 1. Organizational learning. 2. Problem-based learning. 3. Active learning 4. Leadership. I. Title.
HD58.82.M375 2004
658.3'124—dc22

                                                                    2003023883

FIRST EDITION
First printing 2004

Contents

Preface   vii
Acknowledgments   xi
About the Author   xiii

Chapter 1   Emergence of the Power of Action Learning   1

Part 1   Applying the Six Components of
                 Action Learning

Chapter 2   The Problem   27

Chapter 3   The Group   45

Chapter 4   Questions and Reflection   69

Chapter 5   Action Strategies   89

Chapter 6   Individual, Team, and Organizational Learning   109

Chapter 7   The Coach   133

Part 2   Twelve Steps for Action Learning

Chapter 8   Introducing, Implementing, and Sustaining
                 Action Learning   161

References   197
Index   205

Preface

I recently conducted an action learning workshop for nearly fifty training directors from several departments of the U.S. government. Following a brief overview and demonstration of action learning, the directors formed eight randomly chosen groups and spent the next couple of hours working on problems introduced by members of the group. A volunteer in each group served as the action learning coach. To conclude the action learning workshop, I asked each problem presenter whether he or she had been helped. Every single one responded with an enthusiastic "yes." The volunteer learning coaches were then asked to summarize the activity of their group, and each seemed to outdo the other with wonderful testimonials on how well the group had worked on the problem and the valuable learnings that were shared. Finally, a training director from a table at the front of the room asked me, "Does action learning always work this perfectly?" My response to him and to all readers of this book is, "Yes, it can!"

Based on experience with hundreds of action learning projects over the past ten years, I have become more and more confident that action learning has the power to always be successful. If the key elements of action learning are established and allowed to operate, action learning is amazing in its consistent capacity (a) to effectively and efficiently solve problems and challenges with truly innovative and sustaining strategies, (b) to develop teams that continuously improve their capability to perform and adapt, and (c) to capture, transfer, and apply valuable knowledge at the individual, group, organization, and community levels.

Although action learning has been around since it was introduced by Reg Revans in the coal mines of Wales and England in the 1940s, it is only within the past five years that it has begun sweeping across the world, emerging as the key problem-solving and leadership development program for Global 100 giants such as Boeing, Samsung, and GE; for public institutions such as Fairfax County Public Schools and the U.S. Army; and for small firms and medium-sized firms all over the world. Throughout this book you will discover how these and other organizations have flourished with action learning and are also making action learning successful every time.

Requirements for Success in Action Learning

Briefly described, *action learning* is a remarkably simple program that involves a group of people working on real problems and learning while they do so. Optimizing the probability of success in action learning, however, involves some basic components and norms (ground rules), which form the substance of this book. These components include an important and urgent problem, a diverse group of four to eight people, a reflective inquiry process, implemented action, a commitment to learning, and the presence of an action learning coach. Norms include "questions before statements" and "learning before, during, and after action."

Action learning works well because it interweaves so thoroughly and seamlessly the principles and best practices of many theories from the fields of management science, psychology, education, political science, economics, sociology, and systems engineering. Action learning has great power because it synergizes and captures the best thinking of all group members and enriches their abilities.

Purpose of This Book

Over the past ten years, I have had the opportunity to work with thousands of action learning groups around the world, as well as the good fortune of sharing ideas and best practices with many of the world's top action learning practitioners. The purpose of this book is to share what I have experienced and learned, the exhilaration as well as the challenges. Although action learning is a relatively simple process, the essence of which could fit on a three-by-five card, there are a number of key principles and practices that, as I have discovered, move action learning from good to great, that take it from being a solid organizational tool to a spectacular vehicle for transforming the entire organization.

This book describes each of the components of action learning and why they are necessary for action learning success. Through scores of stories and testimonials, the book clearly illustrates how many organizations have implemented and thrived with action learning. It also shows how any organization can simultaneously and effectively achieve the five primary benefits of action learning, namely, problem solving, leadership development, team building, organizational change, and professional learning.

This book presents the basic elements and principles of action learning as well as the more advanced, more recent innovations within the field of action learning, including the role and questions of the action learning coach, the balance between order and chaos for maximum creativity, and the step-by-step procedures for introducing and sustaining action learning within your organization.

Overview of Book

Chapter 1 provides an overview of action learning, the six basic components, and two key ground rules. It summarizes the five greatest challenges encountered by organizations in today's environment and how action learning enables organizations to respond effectively to those challenges. Chapter 1 also highlights the major contributions of action learning to organizations, groups, and individuals.

Chapters 2 through 7 explore in detail each of the six critical components of successful action learning programs. Chapter 2 identifies the criteria for an action learning *problem,* how it is best introduced and examined, and the differences between single-problem and multiple-problem groups. In Chapter 3 we explore the *group,* including diversity of membership, ideal size, continuity, roles, and characteristics. Chapter 4 introduces the reflective inquiry process and discusses the importance of *questions* as well as the group rule "statements only in response to questions." The problem-solving, goal-framing, strategy-development *action* is covered in Chapter 5, and Chapter 6 examines the individual, team, and organizational *learning* achieved through the action learning process. In Chapter 7, the roles and responsibilities, authority, and questions of the *action learning coach* are described. Chapter 8 presents the twelve steps for introducing, implementing, and sustaining action learning in the organization. Specific strategies for applying each step are offered.

Throughout the book are scores of case examples of groups around the world who have introduced action learning into their organizations. The challenges they faced as well as the successes they experienced are discussed. Finally, there are numerous checklists at the end of each chapter to guide readers in understanding and implementing action learning for themselves.

Action Learning: The Power Tool for the Twenty-First Century

Action learning is truly an exciting and awesome tool for individuals, teams, and organizations struggling for success in the twenty-first century. More and more of us have experienced the power and the benefit of action learning in our lives and in our organizations. It is my hope that many more will be able to share in the wonderful and amazing adventure of action learning. If you apply the principles and practices offered in this book, you too will see how action learning can, indeed, be powerful and successful every time. Good luck!

Acknowledgments

I owe a deep debt of gratitude to so many people not only for this book, but for the action learning opportunities and experiences offered by them that made this book possible. First, I would like to recognize the founding pioneer of action learning, Reg Revans, who inspired me and thousands of others around the world about the power of action learning. Reg died in early 2003, and this book is dedicated to his memory.

There are many other giants in the field of action learning from whom I have learned so much, including Lex Dilworth, Charles Margerison, Victoria Marsick, Verna Willis, Gordon Wills, Eric Sandelands, Richard Teare, Dick Gerdzen, Malcolm Bennison, and John Wicks. Special thanks go to the people at the Global Institute of Action Learning—Kathy Johnson, Steve King, Elise Freedman, Chuck Appleby, Cindy Phillips, and Jennifer Whitcomb—who have worked with me to expand action learning around the world.

I am grateful to the many individuals who offered me the opportunity to develop and improve the action learning model presented in this book, especially to Nancy Stebbins at Boeing, Linda Raudenbush at the U.S. Department of Agriculture, Andy Cole and Beth Fennell at Fairfax County Public Schools, Pierre Gheysens at Caterpillar, Harry Lenderman at Sodexho, Penti Sydanmaanlakka at Nokia, Elizabeth King at Bowne, Frank Andracchi at Constellation, and Eric Charoux at the Mauritius Business School.

I would also like to acknowledge the students of my action learning classes who have taken the message of action learning back to their home countries; Antony Hii in Malaysia, Daisie Yip in Singapore, Viwe Mshontshi in South Africa, Rubens Pessanha in Brazil, Marisa Faccio in Italy, Fumiyo Seimiya and Mayuko Horimoto in Japan, Sung Hae Kim in Hong Kong, Taebok Lee and Myoung Choi in Korea, and my many students in the U.S.: Deborah, Terry, Bea, Colleen, Scot, Trenton, Melissa, among others.

Thanks as well go to friends and colleagues who have offered so much encouragement in my work and research in action learning: Arthur Freedman, Ken Murrell, Robert Krammer, Frank Soffo, Neal Chalofsky, Howard Schuman, Skip Leonard, Clive Watkins, and Keith Halperin.

Special thanks to the people at Davies-Black Publishing who have joyfully and competently helped in every stage of the development of the book; to editors Connie Kallback and Jill Anderson-Wilson as well as Laura Simonds and Lee Langhammer Law. I would also like to express my gratitude to all my friends at Management Concepts, which is co-publishing this book.

Finally, I would like to thank my family: my daughter Emily, who refers to her dad as the "traveling guru of action learning"; my daughter Catherine, who must face fellow teachers in Fairfax County Schools who have been trained in action learning by me; and to my daughter Stephanie, son Chris, and my wife, Eveline, for their wonderful love and support.

About the Author

Michael Marquardt, Ed.D., is professor of human resource development and program director of overseas programs at George Washington University. He also serves as president of Global Learning Associates and director of the Global Institute for Action Learning.

Marquardt has held a number of senior management, training, and marketing positions with organizations such as Grolier, American Society for Training and Development, Association Management Inc., Overseas Education Fund, TradeTec, and U.S. Office of Personnel Management. He has trained more than 75,000 managers in nearly one hundred countries since beginning his international experience in Spain in 1969. His consulting assignments have included Marriott, DuPont, Motorola, Nortel, Alcoa, Boeing, Caterpillar, United Nations Development Program, Xerox, San Miguel, Brookings Institute, Nokia, Constellation, National Semiconductor, Warner-Lambert, Citicorp, Organization of American States, and Singapore Airlines, as well as the governments of Indonesia, Laos, Ethiopia, Zambia, Egypt, Kuwait, Saudi Arabia, Turkey, Russia, Jamaica, Honduras, and Swaziland.

Author of fifteen books, Marquardt has published more than fifty professional articles in the fields of leadership, learning, globalization, and organizational change including *Building the Learning Organization* (selected as Book of the Year by the Academy of HRD), *The Global Advantage, Action Learning in Action, Global Leaders for the 21st Century, Global Human Resource Development, Technology-Based Learning,* and *Global Teams.* He has been a keynote speaker at international conferences in Australia, Japan, England, the Philippines, Malaysia, South Africa, Sweden, Singapore, and India, as well as throughout North America.

Marquardt's achievements and leadership have been recognized though numerous awards including the International Practitioner of the Year Award from the American Society for Training and Development. He presently serves as a senior advisor for the United Nations Staff College in the areas of policy, technology, and learning systems. He is a fellow of the National Academy for Human Resource Development and a co-founder of the Asian Learning Organization Network.

Emergence of the Power of Action Learning

Action learning has quickly emerged as a tool used by organizations for solving their critical and complex problems. It has concurrently become a primary methodology utilized by companies around the world for developing leaders, building teams, and improving corporate capabilities. Action learning programs have become instrumental in creating thousands of new products and services, saving billions of dollars, reducing production and delivery times, expanding customer bases, improving service quality, and positively changing organizational cultures.

Since Reg Revans introduced action learning in the 1940s, there have been multiple variations of the concept, but all forms of action learning share the elements of real people resolving and taking action on real problems in real time and learning while doing so. The great attraction of action learning is its unique power to simultaneously solve difficult challenges and develop people and organizations at minimal costs to the institutions. The rapidly changing environment and unpredictable global challenges require organizations and individuals to both act and learn at the same time.

Global Leadership at Boeing

The Boeing Company, the world's leading aerospace company, is a global market leader in missile defense, human space flight, and launch services, with customers in 145 countries, employees in more than 60 countries, and operations in 26 states. Boeing adopted action learning as the methodology for its Global Leadership Program, since action learning enabled the company to build critical global competencies while solving its most critical problems. Action learning has successfully produced a forum for senior-level executives to learn while being challenged with real corporate issues related to the international environment in which they were placed. ■

What Is Action Learning?

Briefly defined, action learning is a powerful problem-solving tool that has the amazing capacity to simultaneously build successful leaders, teams, and organizations. It is a process that involves a small group working on real problems, taking action, and learning as individuals, as a team, and as an organization while doing so. Action learning has six components, each of which is described below and presented in greater detail over the next six chapters of this book.

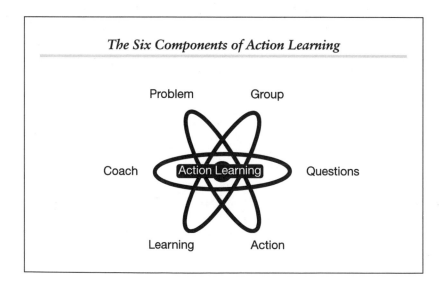

The Six Components of Action Learning

Problem

Group

Coach

Action Learning

Questions

Learning

Action

▲ *A problem (project, challenge, opportunity, issue, or task).* Action learning centers on a problem, project, challenge, opportunity, issue, or task, the resolution of which is of high importance to an individual, team, and/or organization. The problem should be significant and urgent and should be the responsibility of the team to solve. It should also provide an opportunity for the group to generate learning opportunities, to build knowledge, and to develop individual, team, and organizational skills. Groups may focus on a single problem of the organization or multiple problems introduced by individual group members.

▲ *An action learning group or team.* The core entity in action learning is the action learning group (also called a set or team). The group is ideally composed of four to eight individuals who examine an organizational problem that has no easily identifiable solution. The group should have diversity of background and experience so as to acquire various perspectives and to encourage fresh viewpoints. Depending on the action learning problem, group members may be volunteers or be appointed, may be from various functions or departments, may include individuals from other organizations or professions, and may involve suppliers as well as customers.

▲ *A process of insightful questioning and reflective listening.* Action learning emphasizes questions and reflection above statements and opinions. By focusing on the right questions rather than the right answers, action learning focuses on what one does not know as well as on what one does know. Action learning tackles problems through a process of first asking questions to clarify the exact nature of the problem, reflecting and identifying possible solutions, and only then taking action. The focus is on questions, since great solutions are contained within the seeds of great questions. Questions build group dialogue and cohesiveness, generate innovative and systems thinking, and enhance learning results.

▲ *An action taken on the problem.* Action learning requires that the group be able to take action on the problem it is working on. Members of the action learning group must have the power to take action themselves or be assured that their recommendations will be implemented (barring any significant change in the environment or the group's lacking essential information). If the group only makes recommendations, it loses its energy, creativity, and commitment. There is no real meaningful or practical learning until action is taken and reflected on, for one is never sure an idea or plan will be effective until it has been implemented. Action enhances learning because it provides a basis and anchor for the critical dimension of reflection. The action of action learning begins with reframing the problem and determining the goal, and only then determining strategies and taking action.

▲ *A commitment to learning.* Solving an organizational problem provides immediate, short-term benefits to the company. The greater, longer-term, multiplier benefits, however, are the learnings gained by each group member and the group as a whole, as well as how those learnings are applied on a systems-wide basis throughout the organization. Thus, the learning that occurs in action learning has greater strategic value for the organization than what is gained by the immediate tactical advantage of early problem correction. Accordingly, action learning places the same emphasis on the learning and development of individuals and the team as it does on the solving of problems, for the smarter the group becomes, the quicker and better will be its decision-making and action-taking capabilities.

▲ *An action learning coach.* Coaching is necessary for the group to focus on the important (i.e., the learnings) as well as the urgent (i.e., resolving the problem). The action learning coach helps the team members reflect on both what they are learning and how they are solving problems. Through a series of questions, the coach enables group members to reflect on how they listen, how they may have reframed the problem, how they give each other feedback, how they are planning and working, and what assumptions may be shaping their beliefs and actions. The learning coach also helps the team focus on what they are achieving, what they are finding difficult, what processes they are employing, and the implications of these processes. The coaching role may be rotated among members of the group or may be assigned to one person for the duration of the group's existence.

Action learning power is at its peak when all six of these components are in operation. Some organizations employ variations of action learning that utilize fewer than these six components, but to the extent that they do, they lose much of the potential of action learning, not only in the problem solving but also in the individual, team, and organizational development aspects. The difference in using five components, for example, would be like five squared (or twenty-five) versus six squared (thirty-six) if all six elements were employed, or a more than 30 percent decrease in the power of the action learning process. Optimizing the power and ensuring the success of action learning requires all six of these elements, interweaving and reinforcing each other.

Leadership Development at Shell Through Action Learning

Shell utilizes action learning programs to improve the abilities and thinking of leaders in three specific skill areas:

▲ Skills in business-oriented thinking, change management, and implementing change

▲ Team skills, including how to create and manage effective teams

▲ Analytical and synthesizing skills in areas such as finance, marketing, and operations ■

Single-Problem and Multiple-Problem Action Learning Groups

Action learning groups may be formed for the purpose of handling either a single problem or several problems. Table 1 provides an overview of the distinction between single-problem (also referred to as in-company action learning) and multiple-problem (often called open-group or "classic" action learning) programs. Organizations may choose either or both types of action learning approaches, although the single-problem form of action learning is much more popular in corporate settings. The multiple-problem approach tends to be used when individuals from many different environments voluntarily choose to come together to help one another.

In the *single-problem* group, all the group members focus their energies on solving a single problem. In this type of action learning, both the group membership and the problem are determined by the organization. The primary purpose of the group is to solve the problem proposed to them by the organization. The group may disband after handling just one problem or may continue for a longer, indefinite period of time and work on a series of challenges submitted to them by the organization. Membership in the action learning group is determined by the organization and is based on the type of problem and the aims of the program. For example, if the organization is seeking to create networks across certain business units, members from those units will be appointed. If the development of high-potential leaders is the goal, then such leaders will be placed in these

Table 1	*Two Types of Action Learning Programs*
Single-problem or in-company programs	Multiple-problem (open-group or "classic") programs
Entire group works on single problem	Group works on multiple problems
Problem determined by organization	Problems selected by members
Organization commits to take action	Individuals commit to take action
Membership determined by organization	Members self-select
Membership remains intact until disbanded	Members who depart may be replaced
Reflective inquiry process is used	Reflective inquiry process is used
Focus is on both action and learning	Focus is on both action and learning
Group recommends and/or implements	Individual implements the action
Coach may be rotated or permanent	Coach is usually rotated among members

action learning programs. If the issue is more focused, then participants may be selected according to their interests, experience, and/or knowledge. In some in-company action learning programs, individuals may be allowed to volunteer, but the organization reserves the right to confirm or not confirm the final composition of an action learning group.

In *multiple-problem* (open-group or "classic" action learning) sets, each member brings his or her problem/task/project to the group to be solved with the help of fellow group members. Individuals self-select to join the group and support and assist each other with the problems they bring. During action learning sessions, each member is allocated time for the group to work on his or her problem. Thus, a six-member group that meets for three hours would devote approximately thirty minutes to each person's problem. In open-group action learning, the members may meet on a monthly basis for a few months or a few years. Open-group action learning is usually voluntary and has more limited funding. Thus the groups often meet on their own time and rotate the coaching role among themselves. Over a period of time, new members may join as older members withdraw. The members are usually from a variety of organizations as well as independent consultants and people who are no longer in the workplace.

Balancing Chaos and Order in Action Learning

Fully optimizing the power of action learning involves capturing both the flexibility and chaos of action learning (elements such as diversity of membership, complex challenges, creative questions, lack of familiarity with problem and/or context) and the practical, time-urgent structure and order of action learning (elements such as real problems, accountability and responsibility, careful listening, testing, and action). Action learning allows for a wide latitude of processes that encourage innovation while maintaining minimal, but crucial, guidelines, norms, and group ground rules that produce sound, practical, and workable results.

Organizational theorists have recently discovered the importance of what is called the "edge of chaos," or "a natural state between order and chaos, a grand compromise between structure and surprise" (Collier and Esteban, 1999). It is the place where maximum creativity and possibility exist and learning best occurs (Battram, 1999), where a team or organization is optimally responsive to the complexity of the environment but still structured sufficiently to succeed. Fulmer (2000) argues that for a team to succeed, it needs to walk the fine line between stability and change, that is, to stay poised on the edge of chaos.

Successful action learning teams blend limited structure around responsibilities and priorities with extensive communication (listening carefully, asking questions, hearing all perspectives, and so on) and design freedom. Limited structure helps group members make sense of complex problems and operate within a complicated environment. Clear autonomy, communications, and responsibilities enable the group to move forward and apply appropriate solutions (Brown and Eisenhardt, 1998). To stay at the edge of chaos, the team needs a few simple rules and a minimum set of norms or guidance. The rules should be simple but also adaptable (Olson and Eoyang, 2001).

Action learning seeks to avoid too much structure, which would lead to rigidity, constraint, and suppression of needed information and would constrict innovation and the team's ability to adapt. On the other hand, providing too little structure will lead to disorder, lack of focus, and fragmentation, and the group may become too permeable to disruptive input, making the group and its projects too difficult to coordinate.

At the first meeting of the action learning group, norms and group ground rules, which provide clear responsibilities and priorities, are established. The structure and stability in action learning come about as a result of the six components of all action learning programs and the group ground rules (norms established for all action learning

---

Applying Creative Ideas and People with Action Learning at Heineken

Gerard van Schaik, former Chairman of Executive Board

Real progress in business is achieved only by corporations and individuals trying out creative ideas and making them work, by pooling talent, and most of all, by learning while doing. Action learning is the vehicle for achieving this.

---

groups). This structure is counterbalanced by the group's freedom and flexibility, the encouragement of fresh questions, the use of diverse people with and without familiarity with the problem or context. As Dixon (1996) notes, a few firm, clear rules and structure agreed to up front allow for great flexibility later on.

Two Group Norms/Ground Rules That Empower Action Learning

The need to balance chaos and order explains why action learning, with its great flexibility and search for innovation, needs clarity and stability. Since the power of action learning is based on two key behaviors—reflective inquiry and continuous learning—establishing the following two ground rules to help ensure that these fundamental tenets of action learning are practiced is critical for success.

Statements Should Be Made Only in Response to Questions

Since questions provide so many benefits, as will be illustrated in Chapter 4, this action learning ground rule helps group members make the important transition from advocacy to inquiry. This ground rule does not prohibit the use of statements; as a matter of fact, there may still be more statements than questions during the action learning meetings, since every question asked may generate one or more responses from each of the other members of the group, or up to five to ten statements per question.

However, requiring people to think "questions first" transforms the dynamics of the group. The natural impulse to make statements and judgments gives way to listening and reflecting. Once the problem or task has been introduced to the group, the members must first ask questions to clarify the problem before jumping into statements to solve the problem. In action learning, we recognize that there is almost a direct correlation between the number and quality of questions and the eventual final quality of the actions and learnings. Balancing the number of questions and the number of statements leads to dialogue, which is a proper balance between advocating and inquiring.

The Action Learning Coach Has Power to Intervene

Action learning coaches focus all their energy and attention on helping the group learn; they are not involved in working on the problem. They look for opportunities to enhance the learning of the group so that its ability to solve the problem and develop innovative action strategies is increased. The well-known axiom that says the "urgent drowns out the important" (also called the "tyranny of the urgent") underscores the necessity of ensuring that the important will not be forgotten or neglected. Accordingly, if power is not provided to the person who is focusing on the learning, the urgency of the problem will always win out over the importance of the learning. To ensure that learning is maximized for the group, action learning coaches must have the power to intervene whenever they believe there is an opportunity for the group to learn, to improve on what it is not going well, and to continue behaviors that are conducive to solving the problem.

This ground rule indicates, therefore, that when the action learning coach decides to intervene, the group will temporarily stop working on the problem, listen to the questions of the action learning coach (who only asks questions), and respond to those questions. And only when the learning coach has finished asking questions should the group resume working on the problem solving. It is vital that the action learning coach be careful and economical in the timing of and time taken for interventions. Coaches should be cognizant of the fact that group members will be subconsciously continuing to work on the problem during a coaching intervention and, when returning to the problem, will be rejuvenated and more creative than before the intervention.

The action learning coach also controls the ending of a session and thus lets the group know in advance when the time for the problem solving or action planning will end. She then uses the last ten minutes or so to capture the learnings of that session and how these learnings might be applied to individuals, a team, and the organization.

Once a group has been involved in action learning for a short time, the group members truly appreciate these two ground rules and quickly recognize the enormous benefit they provide to the group.

These rules ensure that the *important* elements of learning and questioning occur and thus better enable the group to succeed with the *urgency* of the problem. In short, these two ground rules immensely enhance and expand the power of action learning.

Why Action Learning Works So Well

Action learning has an amazing capacity and power to solve complex problems and change individuals, teams, and organizations. What accounts for this marvelous capacity? Why does action learning work so well? Simply stated, action learning is successful and powerful because it has the unique ability to interweave a wide array of organizational, psychological, sociological, educational, and political theories that form a foundation and synergy unavailable in any other source. Action learning works so well because it integrates and builds on the best practices and principles of the following disciplines:

▲ *Management science.* Action learning incorporates the leadership principles and theories espoused by theorists and world-renowned authors such as Collins, Drucker, Peters, Goleman, and Sashkin. It integrates theories of organizational change and complex adaptive systems as well as the major management principles developed by Maslow, McGregor, and McClelland.

▲ *Education.* Action learning capitalizes on the theories, principles, and practices of each of the five schools of adult learning, namely, the behavioral, cognitive, humanist, social learning, and constructivist schools. Unlike most development programs, which tend to favor one approach or another to learning, action learning bridges these schools and builds from their best ideas and practices.

▲ *Psychology.* Action learning utilizes key aspects of individual, group, social, and organizational psychology, including the classic theories of Jung, Skinner, Rogers, and Mead.

▲ *Group dynamics.* Action learning incorporates the best and most applicable principles of group interaction, communications, cohesion, management of conflict, decision making, strategy development, and action implementation (Sundstrom et al., 1999).

▲ *Sociology.* Action learning taps into the principles of the field of sociology. Also, the benefits gained by having diversity in organizational rank, age, gender, education, and experience allow a group's action learning to be powerful (Weick, 1995).

▲ *Open systems and engineering (chaos theory).* Action learning avoids the limitations of Newtonian physics and uses the energy and chaos of opens systems engineering (Gharajedaghi, 1999). Action learning groups are forced into systems thinking via the questioning process and the diversity in membership.

▲ *Political science.* Action learning utilizes and balances the politics of power, distributing it throughout the group and ensuring opportunities for all to participate and lead. For example, a key power in action learning is not necessarily the person with the highest rank or the most knowledge but rather the one who has the best questions (which may come from a secretary as easily as a CEO).

▲ *Appreciative inquiry.* Action learning searches to uncover and build on the best and most positive elements of every situation. Groups explore first what is going well, what works, what can be done better, what the group wants to achieve—not what went wrong. The group moves quickly from the presenting problem to the reframed problem to what it is attempting to achieve (Cooperrider, Sorensen, and Yaeger, 2001).

▲ *Ethics.* In action learning, issues that are normally kept underneath the table and are used to keep the group from its optimum performance are brought above the table by the questions of the action learning coach. Hidden and political agendas are opened with dialogue rather than entrenched and enhanced with debate and power grabs.

▲ *Biology and life science.* As an organism's environment becomes more complex and unpredictable, the organism must develop adaptive and transformative capabilities. The organism's own capabilities interact with the environment to produce a unique path of evolution. No change can happen that doesn't build on existing capacity. Organisms, like action learning teams, must have the ability to create their own breakthroughs. All parts of the organism must be mobilized for action as action learning carries its learnings to the organization (McLagan, 2003).

▲ *Anthropology.* Action learning is widely practiced and highly effective in cultures around the world because it builds on the universals of humankind and yet is sensitive to individual cultures (Hofstede, 1991; Trompenaars, 1994).

It is action learning's remarkable ability to harness the powers of each of the disparate disciplines that enables it to achieve multiplex purposes of problem solving, team building, organizational learning, leadership development, and professional improvement.

I have found the answer that I have spent my business life searching for!
—Malaysian CEO, upon completion of action learning project

Overview of the Stages of Action Learning

There are many different forms of action learning. Action learning groups may meet for one or several times over a few days or over several months, may handle one or many problems, and may meet for short periods or long periods. Generally, however, action learning occurs via the following stages and procedures:

▲ *Formation of group.* The group may be appointed or made up of volunteers and may be working on a single organizational problem or each other's individual problems. The group will continue for a predetermined amount of time and number of sessions, or it may determine these at the first meeting.

▲ *Presentation of problem or task to group.* The problem (or problems, if a multiproblem group) is briefly presented to the group. Members ask questions to gather more information about the problem or task.

▲ *Reframing the problem.* After a series of questions, the group, often with the guidance of the action learning coach, will reach a consensus as to the most critical and important problem that the group should work on and will establish the crux of the problem, which may differ from the original presenting problem.

▲ *Determining goals.* Once the key problem or issue has been identified, the group searches for the goal, the achievement of which would solve the reframed problem for the long term with positive rather than negative consequences for the individual, team, or organization.

▲ *Developing action strategies.* Much of the time and energy of the group will be spent on identifying and pilot testing possible action strategies. As in the preceding stages of action learning, strategies are developed via the reflective inquiry and dialogue mode.

▲ *Taking action.* Between action learning sessions, the group as a whole, as well as individual members, collects information, identifies status of support, and implements the strategies developed and agreed to by the group.

Action Learning at LG Electronics

Taebok Lee, LGE Consultant, and Eunju Park, LGE Director

LG Electronics (LGE), a major global company specializing in electronics and telecommunications, has seventy-two subsidiaries around the world and more than 55,000 employees. The LGE Learning Center develops and conducts numerous programs to strengthen executive and employee competencies. Its "Global Marketer" program, which employs the action learning approach, seeks to develop global leaders in marketing as well as enable participants to acquire the capabilities to solve any possible problems that they may face in a complex and rapidly changing environment.

Each action learning team is composed of three LG managers, an MBA student from a foreign university, a Korean expert, a foreign expert, and an executive who has specific knowledge and experience. The teams are given a marketing task that has been sponsored by the organization. Examples of group projects include "how to improve brand equity" and "how to launch new products." The teams work on the tasks for two-and-a-half months—one-and-a-half months in Korea and one month overseas. Teams participate in seminars conducted by domestic and foreign experts as well as conduct on-site interviews and surveys with competitors, customers, suppliers, and best practice companies. At the end of the program, each team presents its recommendations to the sponsors and other executives for adoption or adaptation and then implementation. LGE sees action learning as a great success because it has contributed greatly to business performance as well as to the personal development of the participants, including developing their problem-solving and global leadership skills and reinforcing global perspectives.

▲ *Capturing learnings.* Throughout and at any point during the session, the action learning coach may intervene to ask the group members questions that will enable them to reflect on their performance and to find ways to improve their functioning as a group.

Throughout the remaining chapters of the book, we will explore in much greater detail these stages and processes of action learning.

Five Major Challenges Facing Organizations

Organizations are turning to action learning because of its unique and wonderful ability to respond to what most leaders consider to be the five greatest challenges facing organizations in the twenty-first century.

Increased Complexity of Organizational Problems

Today's world is marked by rapid globalization and fierce competition in the marketplace, with turbo-speed changes created by technology. The constant movement of people in and out of organizations has generated sometimes overwhelming complexity and chaos in the workplace. Problems are becoming ever more difficult, require greater innovation, and must be resolved in shorter time periods with larger networks of collaborators. The old ways of solving problems by the single leader or specialized task forces no longer work.

Need for New Leadership Attributes and Capabilities

A new kind of leadership is needed in this competitive, global, knowledge-driven time. Leadership books point to a need for leaders with transformational abilities, strong learning skills, emotional intelligence, ethical standards, problem-solving and project management strengths, keen self-awareness, and humble yet confident capabilities. Few leaders possess all these skills, and traditional executive development programs are unable to offer training programs that build these competencies.

Increased Importance of Effective, High-Performing Teams

More and more of the work of organizations can be done only with teams, since only teams have the knowledge and resources to understand and develop the services and products needed by internal and external customers. Unfortunately, most teams in most organizations are dysfunctional and rarely develop and deliver within the limited times imposed by the marketplace.

Increased Need to Capture and Transfer Valued Knowledge

Knowledge is the most valuable asset of organizations today. Most knowledge, however, remains hidden with an individual or group, and is not transferred to other parts of the organization that can benefit from it. Companies are generally weak in their ability to learn from successes and failure, and knowledge and learning are rarely transmitted and applied in a comprehensive and systematic manner.

Greater Need for Learning and Less Time for It

The constant stream of new products, services, customers, alliances, suppliers, policies, technology, and legislation requires us to learn on a continuous basis. Although we need more and more learning and training, the irony is that we have less time to acquire it. When we do attend a training program or conference, we are so pressured to continue serving our customers or fellow workers that we must spend our coffee breaks and lunch times checking e-mails or answering phone messages. If we are absent from our desks and customers for more than a few hours, the cell phone begins ringing. We need to be constantly in action and working yet constantly learning. We know that we need to drain the swamp (that is, develop our knowledge and abilities), but we are so busy fighting alligators (handling the day-to-day crises) that we never get time to do the draining. In short, we know that we need to learn so we can do our jobs more efficiently and effectively, but we are too busy to find the time to do so.

Action Learning Responds Effectively to These Challenges

Action learning has the matchless power to overcome each of these five major challenges in an effective and cost-efficient manner. To respond to the challenges, action learning enables organizations to simultaneously solve problems, develop leaders, build teams, create learning organizations, and increase individuals' professional skills.

Problem Solving

Action learning begins with and builds around solving problems; the more complex and the more urgent, the better suited is action learning. The dynamic, interactive process used in action learning allows the group to see problems in new ways and to gain fresh perspectives on how to resolve them. Questioning from multiple perspectives creates solid systems thinking in which the group sees the whole rather than parts, relationships rather than linear cause-effect patterns, underlying structures rather than events, and profiles of changes rather than snapshots. The action learning process enables the group to look for underlying causes and leveraged actions rather than symptoms and short-term solutions. Action learning examines both macro and micro views so as to discover when and how to best implement the proposed actions. As a result of its fresh approach to problem solving, action learning generates "breakthrough" insights, solutions, and effective strategies.

Solving Problems for National Semiconductor and AT&T

Working in action learning teams is seen as a key to increasing productivity and creativity at National Semiconductor. When senior managers in the South Portland, Maine, plant saw that delivery performance was holding National Semiconductor back from providing quality service at AT&T, they decided to do something about it. Choosing eight people from different areas throughout the company, they created a Customer Request Improvement Team to deal with delivery performance. Team members were chosen from sales, marketing, engineering, manufacturing, and planning as well as from AT&T. Meeting for two days a month for three months, the team eventually came up with a list of almost forty ideas, which resulted in four key action initiatives:

▲ Analyzing in new ways the delivery misses
▲ Increasing frequencies of lead-time updates
▲ Creating critical device lists
▲ Developing pre-alert reports

Following the implementation of these initiatives, AT&T recognized National Semiconductor as one of its "world-class" suppliers. ■

Leadership Development

Most leadership development programs, whether corporate or academic, have been ineffective and expensive (Pfeffer and Fong, 2002). The weaknesses of traditional leadership development programs are caused by a number of factors, most notably: teachers rather than practitioners are the purveyors of knowledge; a separation exists between the learning and action; very little learning gets transferred to the workplace; the business environment is changing so fast that the knowledge gained from the programs comes too slowly and is inadequate; and there is an absence of reflective thinking in the education process (McNulty & Canty, 1995). Typical executive development programs provide little of the social and interpersonal

---

Action Learning at Dow Chemical

Larry Washington, VP, Human Resources

In today's fast-paced, highly competitive business world, having knowledge-able leaders at every level is our only true competitive advantage. We have found that action learning is the best way to align and motivate our organization to leverage that knowledge for competitive advantage.

---

aspects of the organizations and tend to focus on tactical rather than strategic leadership.

Action learning differs from normal leadership training in that its "primary objective" is to ask appropriate questions in conditions of risk, rather than to find answers that have already been precisely defined by others—and that do not allow for ambiguous responses because the examiners have all the approved answers (Revans, 1982a). Action learning does not isolate any dimension from the context in which managers work; rather it develops the whole leader for the whole organization. What leaders learn and how they learn cannot be dissociated from one another, for how one learns necessarily influences what one learns (Dilworth, 1998).

Learning via traditional leadership programs that use case studies is like learning how to steer a boat by looking out the stern. Examining what happened yesterday will not drive change or make a company competitive. Success factors keep changing, and no company can stay on top by doing what it used to do. In action learning, we have the opportunity to grow as leaders because we are reflecting on what is urgent and important to us and because our assumptions are challenged. McGill and Beaty (1995) point out that action learning provides managers with the opportunity to take "appropriate levels of responsibility in discovering how to develop themselves" (p. 37).

Building Teams

Action learning teams are extremely cohesive and high performing; they become more effective every time they meet because the action learning process focuses on how individually and collectively teams can become smarter and faster. A "teamthink and teamlearn" capability steadily emerges. The group shares clear responsibility and account-

---

Using Action Learning for Building Teams at Siemens

Peter Pribilla, Corporate Human Resources

Building teams has become a key goal and achievement of action learning at Siemens. Action learning has helped the company maximize the entrepreneurial spirit and enhance team player qualities such as cooperation and free exchange of ideas. The teamwork and global networking are designed to reinforce our pro-customer orientation and to optimize knowledge sharing throughout the company. The quality of teams has resulted in more innovative ways of finding new solutions for customer requirements.

---

ability on real problems, causing a need for deliberative team unity and success. The process of ongoing questioning and shared learning builds powerful caring and cohesion among the members. Developing consensus around problems and goals develops clearness of task, strong communications, collaboration, and commitment, during which powerful team synergy and learning emerges.

Creating Learning Organizations

A learning organization is constructed around four primary subsystems: (1) increased learning skills and capacities, (2) a transformed organizational culture and structure, (3) an involvement of the entire business chain in the learning process, and (4) enhanced ability to manage knowledge. Members of action learning groups transfer their experiences and new capabilities to their organizations in a number of ways.

First, action learning groups themselves are mini–learning organizations that model perfectly what a learning organization is and how it should operate. Action learning groups seek to learn continuously from all their actions and interactions. They adapt quickly to external and internal environmental changes. Learning and knowledge are continuously captured and transferred to other parts of the organization that could benefit from the experiences. Individuals who participate in action learning groups appreciate the tremendous benefit of questions and reflection in helping them to continuously improve when they return to their respective jobs. They are better learners as well as better leaders. As the action learning members resume their day-to-day activities, their new mind-sets and skills gradually affect the entire organization, resulting in a culture more likely to continuously learn, reward learning, and connect learning to all business activities.

Building a Learning Organization at WCB

The Workers Compensation Board (WCB) of Alberta is a quasi-judicial insurance company consisting of approximately 1,400 employees. In the last six years, this organization has gone from having a large unfunded liability to one that has a considerable financial surplus. The financial turnaround from deficit to surplus is regarded as an important milestone in the organization's history. However, financial success in an organization does not always translate into high employee morale. New programs were needed—programs to help break down some of the organizational hierarchy, to address morale and retention issues, and to help to build business literacy.

WCB's Leadership in Action Program was designed for managers and supervisors to learn and develop leadership capability through working and taking action on real work projects. Participants cascaded what they learned to colleagues and staff, and also publicized their own successes and the successes of the initiative. At the end of the program, action learning teams presented their achievements and what they had learned to senior management. This ceremonial close to the action learning program had an educational impact on the participants as well as on the audience. For the senior management audience, it was an opportunity to gain exposure to the full spectrum of the organization, as the program participants from all divisions gave five-minute presentations on their projects. The ceremonies also helped to bring about some culture change by providing a positive story in the organization. Learning was seen as an investment rather than as an expenditure. Action learning alumni continue to talk about the confidence they have gained as a result of the program and how they have seen the organization change. (Bowerman and Peters, 2000) ■

Individual Professional Growth and Development

Weinstein (1995) notes that participants in action learning achieve learning at three different levels: (1) understanding something intellectually, (2) applying a newly acquired skill, and (3) experiencing and thereby undergoing an inner development that touches on beliefs and attitudes and leads to personal development. Action learning is particularly effective at this third level since it provides the opportunity for internal dissonance, while the problem and/or action may provide the external trigger. In action learning we become more aware of our blind spots and weaknesses as well as our strengths; and we receive the feedback and help that we have requested.

Action learning generates tremendous personal, intellectual, psychological, and social growth. Butterfield, Gold, and Willis (1998) note that action learning participants experience "breakthrough learning" when they become aware of the need to reach beyond their conscious beliefs and to challenge their assumptions about their present worldviews. This readiness to change and grow is a prerequisite for development. Some of the specific skills and abilities developed for those participating in action learning include:

▲ Critical reflection skills, which are key to *transformative* learning for the individual (Mezirow, 1991)
▲ Inquiry and questioning abilities, which allow the individual to do more than just advocate and push personal opinions
▲ Systems thinking, which helps individuals to see things in a less linear fashion
▲ Ability to adapt and change
▲ Active listening skills and greater self-awareness
▲ Empathy, the capacity to connect with others, which, according to McGill and Beaty (1995), is one of the most valuable relationship skills developed in action learning
▲ Problem-solving and strategy-selection skills
▲ Presentation and facilitation skills

Action learning has also been utilized as a highly valuable tool for examining and advancing one's personal career. For example, job seekers have effectively used action learning to help them better understand themselves, their career goals, their strengths, and the best resources for locating and landing a job.

Action Learning in South Africa

National Sorghum Breweries was regarded by some as a sleepy, money-losing state-owned brewer of traditional African beers. Through a companywide action learning program, the company improved the organization's vision, which revitalized and empowered the organization's employees. Key issues addressed by action learning were the social, political, and economic disadvantages for black South Africans in the wake of apartheid. Action learning groups developed a plan to turn National Sorghum Breweries into a successful company largely owned and managed by black people. The successful privatization of the enterprise and the pride it gave to the black community was seen as one of the early successes in the postapartheid era. ■

Action Learning Differs from Other Problem-Solving Methods

Problem-solving groups are similar to action learning groups in that both involve a group of people who work on a problem and try to solve it. Similarly, we could say that a caterpillar and a butterfly are alike in that they are composed of the same organic elements. We all would agree, however, that there are great differences between the butterfly and caterpillar. Through a metamorphosis, the caterpillar has transformed those organic elements into a new organism that has much greater power and capabilities that allow it to fly up and down, backward and forward, fast and slow. Through this transformation, the butterfly survives and succeeds. In a similar vein, action learning, with its speed and power and intelligence, completely transforms the capability of the problem-solving process and group.

Although problem-solving groups, whether quality circles or task groups and committees, may employ many of the six action learning components, *none* of them applies all six components and the two ground rules of action learning. Here's how each of the six components of action learning together creates and weaves a new kind of problem-solving power.

Problem

The problems in action learning are critical, complex, and urgent to the organization, team, or individual. They are not case studies or unimportant problems, but challenges needing real actionable results. Complicated problems are presented briefly so as to allow the action learning process to identify the most strategic problem to be resolved.

Group

The membership size is fixed between four and eight (not the ten or more found in some groups). Members are sought for their diverse perspectives and characteristics rather than for their expertise or rank in the organization. Diversity is deemed more valuable than expertise for solving complex problems and developing new individual, team, and organizational knowledge and competencies.

Questions

Most problem-solving groups begin with various members offering solutions. Questions are rarely heard, but statements and advocacy are rampant. In action learning, questions and reflection are the mainstays of working on and solving the problem. Finding the great question is the key task and skill of the group. Reflective inquiry more quickly leads to consensus and quality of actions.

Action

Action learning groups exist for the purpose of determining actions that they or the organization will be taking. They do not merely make recommendations. Because they are the only people working on the particular problem, they are accountable and responsible for achieving a breakthrough solution. Reframing the problem precedes identification of strategies. Action is not only important for its own sake, but also to provide opportunities for learning.

Learning

In action learning, the learning is as important as, if not more important than, the successful solution of the problem. Everyone in the group has acknowledged that he or she must seek to learn as well as seek solutions. Time and energy are spent at all sessions to capture individual, team, and organizational learnings.

Coach

To ensure that learning receives its proper level and time, a person is designated whose only responsibility is to assist and enable the group to capture and leverage its learnings. When this person intervenes, the group pauses to examine its progress and learnings and to identify what will make the group more effective as a team as well as individually and organizationally.

Action Learning at Oxford University Press

Oxford University Press (OUP) has been in existence for more than five hundred years and employs some five hundred people. The new UK Publishing Services managing director, David Fry, was particularly concerned to open up the OUP culture, to sharpen up service provision, and to reduce costs—but not necessarily at the expense of people while increasing revenues. The challenge was to find a tool that would include cultural change, people development, and a bottom-line contribution to OUP, a tool that would not just tinker with processes, but would bring about significant long-term change. OUP discovered and applied action learning, which accomplished the following:

▲ Helped managers learn the skills they needed to manage a real business-related project with clearly defined deliverables

▲ Encouraged the delegation of tasks and empowerment of staff

▲ Identified tangible rewards and satisfaction plus measurable financial gains in completing the projects

▲ Promoted teamwork and encouraged cross-functional work

▲ Spread knowledge of the company's aims and objectives

▲ Created a positive—not a blame—culture (Marsh and Wood, 2001) ■

Success with Action Learning

Action learning is a magiclike tool that has revolutionized how organizations around the world solve problems and handle crises. It has become the methodology of choice for developing leaders and building high-performance teams. Individuals have transformed the manner in which they work and live their lives.

Yet this remarkable tool is so basic and simple and built on common sense that it is easily able to be applied by individuals and teams to every corner of our organizational and professional lives. Six basic components and two key ground rules create all the necessary conditions for innovatively solving problems and developing people. Action learning groups can be oriented and operational within an hour. Action learning coaches can be effective by carefully asking a series of development-related questions. Many of the success stories told in this book were achieved the first time the organization initiated an action learning program. The following chapters of the book will highlight and exemplify how you can use action learning to reach similar heights of success in your organization.

Applying the Six Components of Action Learning

The Problem

The starting point for action learning is the problem (also referred to as a project, challenge, opportunity, issue, or task), the resolution of which is of high importance to an individual, team, and/or organization. Simply put, without the problem, there can be no action learning. The problem should be important, urgent, significant, and within the responsibility of the team, and should provide an opportunity for the group to learn. The more complicated the problem, the more innovative becomes the action learning solution and the greater the degree of learning.

With action learning, problems are seen not only as a challenge, but also as an opportunity for learning and for developing individual, team, and organizational abilities. Problems are not burdens, but occasions to sharpen the wit as well as the skills of the people facing the problem. A fundamental premise of action learning is that we learn best when undertaking an action, which we then reflect on and learn from. The problem or project gives the group something to focus on that is real, important, and relevant; it means something to the group. It offers an opportunity to test stored-up knowledge.

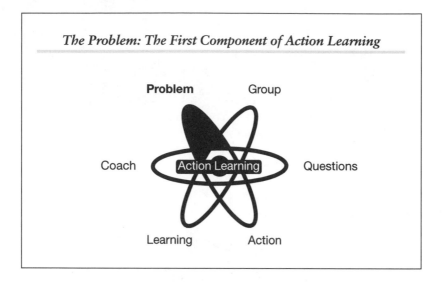

The Problem: The First Component of Action Learning

Using the Term Problem

Problem is a word with many different meanings—*difficulty, quandary, trouble, dilemma, crisis,* and *predicament* are among the synonyms listed in a thesaurus. Some people use *challenge, task, project,* or *opportunity* instead. Although these words do convey what the group is working on, action learning leaders prefer the term *problem* because it better captures a sense of urgency and critical need for resolution. A problem generates a healthy pressure on the group, which leads to greater thinking, action, and learning, all of which are essential to action learning. Although *issue* or *challenge* or *opportunity* may imply an interesting and important matter, these words may not give the group a feeling of seriousness and significance. The excitement and commitment of the group thereby suffer, as does the quality of the solution and learning. ■

Criteria for Choosing the Problem

Not just any problem should be chosen as an action learning problem. The best or *ideal* action learning problems have a number of attributes that optimize the power and value of action learning.

Importance

First and foremost, the problem must be important and critical to the individual or organization that is posing it to the group. Solving the problem should make a significant difference to the individual or organization. The more urgent and more important the problem, the greater will be the energy and excitement and commitment of the group to solve it. If the problem is unimportant or too simple (or perceived as such), the group will not put as much effort and energy into solving it, and their capacity to be an effective problem-solving team will not be tested. In addition, the group may feel that the organization or individual does not have a great deal of confidence or trust in the group. As a result, the time and resources of the group will not be well used, nor will their potential be fully tapped.

Urgency

There must be some degree of urgency to the problem. There should be a real time frame in which the problem needs to be clearly defined and actions developed and taken. The group must know that its ideas and strategies will be acted on by some future date.

No Existing Solution

The problem should not be hypothetical or one that someone or some other organization has. Nor should the problem be merely a puzzle (a problem that has a single correct answer, which has probably already been determined by top management and which the group is expected to reinforce). It must be a true problem, one that has no existing solution and for which different people might come up with different solutions and strategies. And, of course, it should not be a case study, which, according to Revans (1982a), means "edited descriptions by unknown authors of inaccessible conditions for which members cannot deploy the talent of observation."

Problems Given to Groups at Oxford University Press

Projects must not be simply dreamed up by anyone. They have to be real and meaningful. Revans's first principle of action learning projects is: problems not puzzles! In other words, if the problem can be solved easily and does not challenge the individual, then it is not worth the time and trouble for an action learning approach. ■

Feasibility

The problem must be feasible, that is, within the purview or the capability of the organization as well as within the competence of one or more members of the group to understand the problem or the context. If the problem is too complex for the time and resources available or overcomplicated, with too many variables, it will overwhelm rather than challenge the group.

Familiarity

There should be some familiarity for one or more members of the group with the problem and the context of the problem. However, just as it is desirable that someone be familiar with the problem, so is it advisable that not everyone be familiar with it. Total group familiarity can result in less innovative thinking. In addition, there may be less challenging of each other's basic assumptions about the problem. The fewer the members of the group who are familiar with the problem and its context, the greater the likelihood that there will be more innovative solutions. A person unfamiliar with a problem and/or the context in which the problem takes place will be forced to ask fresh questions, which, in turn, will stretch the thinking of the group and ultimately lead to breakthrough solutions. Greater challenges generally generate greater learnings.

Significance

The problem must be important and significant to one or more members of the group. In multiple problem sets, of course, this should not be an issue. In single problem sets, however, it would be possible for this criterion not to be met. However, if the top management has indicated to the entire group or to one or more individuals in the group that their careers, salary, reputation, and/or future opportunities depend on the success of the group's strategies in solving the problem, then the problem will have significance.

Learning Opportunity

The best action learning problems also provide excellent and important learning opportunities for the group, especially learning about issues and skills that are critical to the organization. For example, if the organization would like the group members to learn about some content area such as customer relations, a problem related to that area would be presented to the group. If the development of leadership or team skills (which can be a learning aspect of all action learning groups) is what the organization seeks for the group members, then a problem that would develop those skills would be chosen. If a problem provides few opportunities for significant learning, a great benefit of the action learning process will have been lost. Also, it is important for the individual, team, and/or organization to realize that the greater the challenge in solving the problem, the greater will be the learning opportunities.

Group Authority

Finally, the problem should be one in which the group has been given the authority and power to solve and to implement action. If the group is unable to take action, group members will not know if their ideas, strategies, and learnings really work. And if the group has been notified that it is merely to make recommendations, which may or may not be implemented, the group's energy level will be low, members will be less creative, frustration and/or apathy may arise, and members may skip meetings and not undertake agreed-upon tasks.

Problem Choosing at Boeing

For the Global Leadership Program, careful effort is made to choose real business issues and problems, the resolution of which are essential to Boeing. It is important that we not choose some interesting but unimportant topic around which no action may be taken. Problems chosen should include an array of complexity and challenges that provide greater opportunities for the selected managers to develop an array of leadership competencies. Thus, finding problems with greater learning opportunities is important. ■

Types of Problems Facing Organizations

Many of the problems faced by organizations today are more complex than the problems encountered five or fifteen years ago. The twenty-first-century workplace involves a wide array of rapidly changing socioeconomic trends and markets, highly innovative competitors, mergers among disparate corporate cultures and industries, continually new distribution channels, and the globalization of business. In confronting these complex challenges, leaders will not find ready-made solutions. Problems have become ever more confusing and difficult to identify, much less solve. And solving problems can no longer be the domain of a single person or leader—there is simply too much information to incorporate and too many implications to be considered.

The imagination, perspectives, and talents of many people need to be accessed to find the answers to today's overwhelming dilemmas. No one person, however prescient, will be able to fully understand the problem; nor can any group composed of people with similar backgrounds and perspectives generate the innovative answers that are needed.

Heifetz and Laurie (1997) make a distinction between the problems that were common to the twentieth century and those that are most prevalent and important in the twenty-first century, that is, problems that are *technical* as opposed to problems that are *adaptive* in nature and context.

Technical problems (those more common in the twentieth century) are those in which the necessary knowledge to solve the problem already exists in a legitimized form or set of procedures. The challenge in solving such problems requires the acquisition and application of knowledge in an efficient and rational—or Newtonian—way. Technical problems have linear, logical solutions, with precedents within or outside the organization; they are like puzzles, with single right answers.

Adaptive problems (more and more frequent in the twenty-first century) are problems for which no satisfactory response has yet been developed and no technical expertise is fully adequate. The challenge is to mobilize the people with the problem to make painful adjustments in their attitudes, work habits, basic assumptions, and other aspects of their lives, while at the same time they are learning their way into the creation of something that does not yet exist. Adaptive problems have no ready solutions. Technical expertise is not enough. They require people collectively to apply their intelligence and skills to the work only they can do. They also require people to unlearn the habits of a managerial lifetime, to learn to meet challenges for which current skills are insufficient, and to explore and understand the competing values that are at stake. Adaptive problems are difficult to define and resolve because they require the efforts of people throughout the organization.

This is not to say that technical problems are unimportant or easy to solve. But they are called *technical* because the information and knowledge needed to resolve them already exist, and those in authority have a concrete set of procedures or guidelines to follow as they work through the issues at hand. As the workplace continues to become more complex, however, strategic and operational problems will require more than a technical response. Action learning groups will be faced with learning more adaptive approaches in order to solve problems for which no plan of action has yet been developed and current technical expertise is not fully adequate.

Challenges for Fairfax County School Principals

Over the past two years, the principals and assistant principals of Fairfax County Public Schools in Virginia have worked in action learning teams and effectively explored and developed strategies for numerous challenges. Examples of problems tackled include:

▲ How to deal with angry, demanding parents
▲ How to implement standards of learning (SOL) throughout the school system
▲ How to handle and supervise ineffective teachers
▲ How to develop key aspects of leadership at the FCPS Leadership Institute
▲ How to keep a balance between personal and professional lives
▲ How to deal with continuous "gotta minute" requests and yet stay on top of key management responsibilities
▲ How to make disciplinary decisions, especially when a "good" kid might benefit from alternative consequences as opposed to those imposed by standard school policies ■

Examples of Action Learning Problems

Since Reg Revans first began applying action learning to solve problems in the coal mines of Wales and England, action learning teams have overcome a wide array of difficult problems over the past sixty years. Individuals and organizations of all backgrounds and from every part of the world have achieved marvelous successes in handling challenges from marketing to management, from quality to quasars, from training to technology. Examples of problems posed to action learning groups include:

▲ How to create a billion-dollar service/solutions-based business
▲ How to cut $100 million in costs using Six Sigma
▲ How to recruit and retain high-tech workers
▲ How to teach a French curriculum
▲ How to get an employee to work on time
▲ How to double business in Latin America by 2005
▲ How to overcome regulatory barriers to global growth
▲ How to identify alliance partners and acquisitions
▲ How to capitalize on the network computing phenomenon to reassert leadership and growth
▲ How to develop a risk management strategy for emerging markets
▲ How to better leverage a company's technology to create value for customers
▲ How to improve customer service

▲ How to simplify the manufacturing process by 25 percent

▲ How to resolve conflicts between business units

These and thousands of other types of problems both large and small—and always of significance—represent the potential value of action learning to organizations, groups, and individuals.

Problems and Action Learning at Deutsche Bank

In the late 1990s, Deutsche Bank faced tremendous changes in its business and staff structure, with critical implications for corporate culture. Organizational change was critical, and the following steps were considered:

▲ Reconfiguration along divisional product lines

▲ Shift from regional to global operational structure

▲ Shift from multinational to global leadership structure

▲ Acquisition of several U.S. entities and their leadership model

▲ Change in corporate language from German to English

Developing leadership to handle these challenges was critical. Deutsche Bank recognized, however, that existing leadership development courses were focused on individual, not organizational, development. As a result, little knowledge was transferred to the workplace, nor were new skills applied to business challenges. In addition, the cost of off-the-job training and development was high and climbing. In searching for a tool that would develop leaders while simultaneously resolving these challenges, Deutsche Bank chose action learning because of its just-in-time learning and self-managed learning efficiency.

Key business challenges were identified and a six-month action learning program was begun. The CEO, program director, and/or program manager selected the problems best suited for Deutsche Bank and for the action learning participants. Each problem had to meet four criteria:

▲ Of strategic importance to the bank

▲ Potential source of significant organizational change

▲ Strategic—not tactical—in nature, to "stretch" participants

▲ Broad in scope, offering rich learning opportunities

Twenty participants were selected. Following a two-day introduction to action learning, the four groups met over a period of six to eight weeks on a part-time basis to work on their problems. The final two days of the program included the presentation of actions taken as well as the capturing of learning that could be applied throughout Deutsche Bank. The program was considered a great success, having attained innovative and cost-effective actions for each of the company's problems. ■

Single Versus Multiple Problems in an Action Learning Group

Action learning groups may be formed for the purpose of handling either a single problem or several problems. In the single-problem group (also referred to as in-company action learning), all group members focus all their energies on solving that problem. In multiple-problem sets, each individual brings his or her problem to the group for fellow members to help solve. Organizations tend to choose the single-problem approach, whereas the multiple-problem approach (also referred to as the open-group or "classic" approach) is much more common when individuals from many different environments voluntarily choose to come together to help one another. In Chapter 1, we introduced some of the key distinctions between the two types of action learning. Let us explore in more depth the characteristics and benefits of these two approaches to action learning.

Single-Problem Action Learning

Single-problem action learning groups work on one common problem for the duration of their existence. This problem is generally selected by the organization, which has probably also appointed the membership of the action learning group. The group as a whole is not only responsible for reframing the problem and developing action strategies, but may also be designated to implement the solutions the group has developed. The organization "sponsors" the project/problem and ensures that the organization will be committed to taking action. The single-problem type of action learning offers numerous benefits to the participants and to the organization:

▲ A key, critical organizational problem is being handled in a highly effective way with a wide array of skills and focused energy.
▲ The impact on the organization will be significant, since a number of people from different parts of the organization will develop skills, knowledge, and ways of thinking and working as a team that will have a major impact on the culture of the organization, a foundational step in building a learning organization.
▲ Silos and barriers that might exist in the organization will be broken down as people from several business units who normally do not work together now strive jointly to resolve a critical organizational issue. New and strong networks and collaboration will emerge within the organization.

▲ Group members have the opportunity to demonstrate their leadership potential and other capabilities to the organization, and thus benefit their career advancements as well as the organization's future staffing requirements.

▲ The group skills developed can be applied to the multiple groups that the individual members participate in on a daily basis within the organization. Future staff meetings, for example, will become more productive and efficient.

▲ The problem-solving skills that will be developed will be a valuable asset to the organization for years in the future.

▲ The ability of individuals to continuously reflect and learn while on the job will produce immense dividends in every aspect of organizational life.

Action Learning at New York City Transit

New York City Transit used action learning to handle three major problems of the subway system: increased ridership, unintelligible announcements, and lack of teamwork. Action learning groups composed of the widest possible diversity based on job function, gender, ethnicity, and age were formed. Each action learning group identified five to ten possible solutions, and all but two were implemented. The action learning teams not only solved the problems, but changed the organizational culture as well. (Meyer, 2000) ■

Multiple-Problem Action Learning

The multiple-problem action learning format is one in which each individual member brings his own problem/task/project to the group. The members may be from different departments of the same organization or from different organizations, or they may be simply individuals with a desire to help one another. For example, a group of people who are searching for jobs could help one another clarify career goals, job targets, strategies, and potential resources. In the multiple-problem format, each person serves as both a problem presenter/client and, in turn, as a resource/questioner to the other group members.

At the beginning of each action learning session, the group, with the help of the action learning coach, establishes the time frame so that each person has an agreed-upon time period to receive help and guidance on his or her problem. Generally the time is divided equally among the members, so that if there is a three-hour session, for example, with six members, each member would have approximately thirty minutes to be the focus. During this time, group members ask questions of, support, and challenge each other. Members decide together how often they will meet and where, and for how long a period they intend to work as a group.

At the first meeting members introduce their problems, then receive help reframing the problem and identifying action steps they would need to take to resolve the problem. At the end of his allocated time, the presenter is asked what action he intends to take. Following each individual's session, as well as at the end of the entire session, the action learning coach asks questions to enable the group to reflect on the decisions and interactions of the group and thereby helps the group improve its capabilities as a group. The coach also assists group members with identifying how their learnings can be applied to their respective organizations and/or lives.

At the next meeting, each person, during her allotted time, updates the group as to the actions taken and progress she has made on the problem, what the results were, what new difficulties may have arisen, and what further action she is considering. The group continues working on the problem through subsequent sessions until the individual declares that the problem has been resolved. If the individual's problem has been resolved or is no longer urgent to her, she may introduce a new problem to the group.

The role of the action learning coach may rotate among the individual members or may be taken by an outside person who serves in that role permanently, that is, someone who is not bringing a problem to the group. (See Chapter 7 for a thorough discussion of the roles and options for action learning coaching.)

Just as there are many advantages to the single-problem action learning project, so too are there numerous advantages for individuals and organizations that implement the multiple-problem type of action learning. First and most important, each individual receives undivided attention to his problem and, as a result, gains insights and ideas and solutions for his problem. The help given on this problem may be worth thousands of dollars and/or save hundreds of hours of doubt, frustration, and consternation.

When sharing problems with people who are not within her company or who are not her subordinates, the individual has a greater degree of comfort and freedom to share issues, concerns, personalities, and vulnerabilities than might be possible if the problem were discussed with company colleagues. Issues such as how to handle a subordinate, how to get a boss to recognize one's work, and whether or not to remain with a company are hardly problems that one would want to share inside the organization. Most of us are able to be more open and honest with people who are not working with or for us.

In multiple-problem groups in which members are from different organizations, there may be less hierarchical and fewer political issues to deal with as people work on each other's problems. In addition, when working with people from different organizations, individuals have the advantage of hearing different perspectives and approaches to problems and solutions. They also discover the various ways that other organizations react to and solve similar problems. This may cause individuals to change their mind-sets and set patterns for responding to issues and challenges.

The problems brought forth in multiple-problem sets are generally the personal, heartfelt, and urgent problems faced by individuals, who otherwise may feel alone in trying to resolve the issues. It is satisfying and fulfilling to help others with problems that are important and meaningful to them. Plus, sharing our individual problems with others often results in a meaningful insight—that my problem is not unique, that other people have the same or similar problems, and I am not such a poor manager after all. This awareness provides us with great support and greater self-confidence.

Finally, as we help others with their problems and receive help in ours, we develop a number of important professional and personal competencies, such as how to give and receive feedback and help, how to solve problems, how to listen, how to do systems thinking, how to be more courageous, and how to take risks.

Action Learning at Novartis and Partners

Novartis is a world leader in health care, with core businesses in pharmaceuticals, consumer health, generics, eye care, and animal health. Headquartered in Basel, Switzerland, Novartis employs more than 72,000 people and operates in more than 140 countries around the world. Novartis recently formed a consortium of six noncompetitive companies from different sectors. Each company sends six to eight HR leaders to become part of a consortium action learning group. The resultant six to eight action learning groups (composed of a representative from each company) work as teams on business projects of importance to their respective companies. Each project has a business or HR sponsor from the company. The purposes of the action learning groups are threefold: to solve the business problems of the companies, to develop leaders, and to build organizational capacity. Leadership skills focus on developing a global mind-set, emotional intelligence, leadership style, and business acumen. ∎

Who Presents the Problem?

In the single-problem action learning set, there are a number of possible options regarding who presents the problem and how it is presented to the group. In some situations, the presenter may be either the person who is the true owner of the problem or someone who has been designated by the organization, who will be responsible for having the strategies implemented and who will be a permanent member of the group.

There may be occasions when the true owner will be unable to be present at every meeting of the group (it is very important for each group member to be present at all meetings of the action learning group, as will be discussed in Chapter 3), or he may feel that his presence would lessen the spontaneity and courage of the group in seeking fresh answers or examining root causes to his problem. In these circumstances, the group may ask the problem owner to be present at the first meeting so that they can ask questions that will provide them with a clear picture of the problem as well as secure an understanding of the person's commitment and resources for implementing the group's decisions and strategies.

Sometimes the problem is one in which several or all of the members of the group are themselves currently enmeshed. The individuals who have knowledge of the situation and problem then serve as the resources for providing information the group will need to reframe the problem, develop goals, and plan actions.

In multiple-problem groups, each person is responsible for presenting her problem to the group. New problems may be introduced in subsequent meetings if the earlier problem has been resolved or a newer, more urgent problem has arisen between sessions.

Prince William County

Prince William County, located in the suburbs of Washington, D.C., brought together an action learning team composed of directors of the various departments—police, library, human services, fire, and so forth—to work on the issue of auto decals. The solution was built on the system of how books are loaned by libraries, a solution offered by the librarian. The idea saved money, pleased citizens, and won the annual award for local governments in the State of Virginia. ■

How to Present the Problem to an Action Learning Group

The initial presentation of the problem should be short, with an emphasis on the important points. Pedler (1996) suggests that problem presenters prepare themselves by examining the following questions.

▲ How can you describe your problem situation in a few sentences?
▲ Why is this problem important to you and/or the organization?

▲ How would you recognize progress on this problem?
▲ What are the difficulties you anticipate as you and/or the organization work through this problem?
▲ What will be the benefits if this problem is minimized or resolved?

There are a number of reasons for limiting the introductory presentation of the problem to a few minutes. First, it forces the group to get into the questioning mode, since there is so much information they still need before they can begin working on the problem. A short introduction of the problem also eliminates a lot of the unimportant and extraneous information that the presenter may believe is important, but that may or may not be vital for the group to know. The more voluminous the amount of information that the presenter provides, the more he will "box in" and limit the range of solutions and innovative options that may be possible. Sometimes presenters deliberately provide many details because they want the group to reach the same or a similar solution to the one they have in mind. Oftentimes, however, presenters unintentionally constrain the group. In action learning, the group will systematically and naturally ask the necessary questions and get the information that is essential for solving the problem. A final benefit of minimizing the initial presentation of the problem is that the questions coming from around the group begin to mold them together as a group, as they jointly uncover and discover the real problem.

It is important to note that although initially the questions will tend to be directed to the presenter(s), they should gradually be posed to other members of the group as the group becomes more and more familiar with the problem. Otherwise, the presenter may feel like he is part of an inquisition. The presenter can change this dynamic by doing any of the following: he may indicate that he is unable to answer a particular question at this time, he can say that he needs to reflect on it for a while, or, what is most valuable, he can begin asking questions of the group.

The Presented Problem May Not Be the Critical Problem

Organizational psychologists such as Block (1999) and Vaill (1996) note that the problem originally presented is rarely the problem that is the most critical one for the group to work on; oftentimes it is only a symptom, and a more urgent and important problem emerges as the group works on the original problem. In action learning, groups carefully determine whether solving the original problem really resolves the situation. Gaining clarity and consensus on the real problem is thus the first and most important part of problem solving in action learning, for if we jump into solving the initial problem, we may end up solving the wrong problem.

The original problem is rarely the problem that ends up being addressed. There's something about action learning that allows people to uncover layers to an issue. Too often we apply solutions to surface problems. That's why so many of our problems don't remain solved. When we think we know what the problem is and try to provide a solution (because that is what is expected of us as leaders), we miss an opportunity to examine the issue in all its depth and complexity.
—Terry Carter, action learning participant

Biases in Presenting the Problem

When presenting a problem to a group, we should seek to be accurate and clear. If we do not, it becomes difficult for the group to correctly understand it or adequately resolve it. Many of us often unintentionally filter our presentation with biases and preconceptions such as the following.

▲ *Anchoring and adjustment.* What we choose to present does not come out of the air. It is usually built upon our values and basic assumptions, which determine what we believe is important in the problem and color how we present it.

▲ *Representativeness.* We tend to assess the likelihood of the cause of or the solution to the problem as matching a preexisting category (for example, these kinds of customers always act this way and cause these kinds of problems).

▲ *Recent and past occurrences.* We tend to assume that what has happened in the past will occur again and soon in the future relative to our problem.

▲ *Preconceptions.* We tend to have expectations about the problem and possible solutions that may have little to do with reality.

Thus, it is important to be cognizant of the fact that both the problem presenters and the problem solvers have potential biases and preconceptions when one begins to ask questions about the problem or propose solutions for it.

Problems As Opportunities for Success and Growth

The Chinese word for *crisis* contains two symbols, one denoting danger and the other denoting opportunity. Action learning views problems in a similar light in that problems are indeed both a "hump to get over" and a tremendous opportunity to learn, to grow, to develop skills and competence, to practice, and to perform. The greatest and most significant learnings and achievements have occurred when individuals, teams, organizations, communities, and nations faced seemingly overwhelming problems, such as epidemics, or impossible challenges, such as reaching the moon in ten years. Action learning groups welcome these types of challenges because they are confident that the action learning process will lead to breakthrough solutions.

Checklist for Selection and Presentation of Action Learning Problems

▲ Is the problem significant and important to the organization and/or individual?

▲ Is the problem urgent?

▲ Is there a time frame for taking action?

▲ Is the problem within the scope and feasibility and understanding of one or more group members?

▲ Will the group or a member of the group have authority to take action?

▲ Do we know who will be responsible and accountable for taking the action?

▲ Does the problem provide learning opportunities?

▲ Will the group be handling a single problem or multiple problems?

▲ Has the problem been presented in a brief manner?

▲ Do we acknowledge that the presented problem may not be the real or most important problem for the group to solve?

The Group

The core entity in action learning is the action learning group (sometimes referred to as the "set" or team). The members of the action learning team become the people who are responsible for reframing the problem, determining the most strategic goals, and developing and taking the actions. The action learning group is ideally composed of four to eight individuals with diverse backgrounds and experiences; this diversity provides the wide array of perspectives and fresh viewpoints that ultimately lead to breakthrough thinking. Membership may include individuals from across functions or departments and, when possible and appropriate, from other organizations, professions, and even suppliers or customers.

Selection of Group Members

In determining who will be the members of an action learning group, there are a number of issues and criteria to be considered.

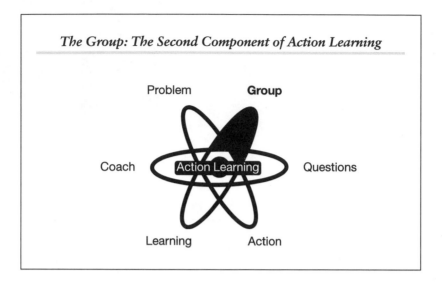

The Group: The Second Component of Action Learning

Problem Group

Coach Action Learning Questions

Learning Action

Commitment

One or more members must have a commitment to and stake in getting this problem solved or task completed. The issue should be one that individuals care about that needs to be resolved for the professional success and/or well-being of the organization, department, group, or individual.

Knowledge

One or more members should have some knowledge and understanding of the problem. Although expertise may be sought from outside the group, it is advisable for the group to have a reasonable amount of knowledge within its membership.

Power to Implement

Ideally the person or persons who have the power to implement the actions should be members of the group. If such a person cannot be part of the group because of other commitments, then it is important that the group members know that either (a) they have the power themselves to implement the strategies they develop or (b) the organization, business unit, and/or person with the power to implement action has assured the group that the strategies proposed by the group will be carried out.

Familiarity

One or more members should be familiar with the context in which the problem resides. There are benefits in having a mix of members in which some are familiar with the context and the problem and some are not. Those with familiarity can provide background and depth to the other members. Individuals who are familiar with the problem, however, may have a more difficult time seeing "outside the box." They often have pre-conceived ideas about the causes of the problem, what will or will not work, why some situations cannot change, and so on. They thus may too quickly reject the fresh ideas of members who have less familiarity with the context or problem. Members unfamiliar with the problem will need more time to "get up to speed," but once they grasp the situation, their new perspectives will result in more outside-the-box thinking and insights that might not have been possible otherwise.

Diversity

Group members may be chosen from all different hierarchical levels of the organization. One of the wonderful attributes of action learning is its potential for individuals of different ranks, education, and experience to work together effectively and on an equal basis. This occurs because asking good questions and listening well are central to action learning success. A janitor or customer or clerk may be able to ask better questions than a manager or CEO; thus, the reflective inquiry process "levels" the hierarchy. Those new to action learning are often amazed at how quickly and easily people of different socioeconomic and academic backgrounds work smoothly and effectively together.

Member Selection

If the organization selects members for action learning groups (as opposed to individuals volunteering), it is key that the company choose carefully and strategically. As Dilworth (1998) points out, membership is an important issue, and selection should not occur randomly. By selecting people from different departments, for example, the organization can not only gain a variety of perspectives and ideas, but also can build organizational learning and connectedness through the creation of networks that did not exist before.

Attendance

Members of an action learning group should be present at all the meetings of the group. The growth, workings, and cohesiveness of an action learning group are different from other types of problem-solving groups. It is much better to schedule fewer meetings when everyone can be present than more meetings when someone might be absent. Members of action learning groups, to amplify the metaphor mentioned in Chapter 1, metamorphose in a special way. Once the members have become butterflies, you do not want them to be joined by those still in the caterpillar phase. Therefore, before or at the first meeting, everyone should identify and commit to the dates and times at which all members can be present.

Size of Action Learning Group

A group size of four to eight members is desirable because it provides sufficient diversity without too much complexity. Having more than eight members creates the following challenges:

▲ *Too little and/or too much participation.* In action learning, active participation by all members is desirable. In groups of more than eight, there is simply not enough time for everyone to remain involved. Individuals either will be aggressive to insert their views or ask their questions, or they will back away and become passive, particularly if their nature is not to be pushy. Group members may not be happy with either choice but may feel they have no other options. And individuals from cultures that value a respectful silence after someone speaks may never be heard.

▲ *Too much complexity of communications.* More than eight people create an enormous complexity of communication patterns. The difference between eight and ten people is the difference between eight squared and ten squared, or sixty-four versus a hundred, possible communication channels. Small group conversations are likely to occur, with judgments and viewpoints being asserted outside the realm of the entire group.

▲ *Too much time needed to reach consensus.* As we know, many problems and tasks must be worked out and decided within a few hours or even less. The more people involved in making a decision, however, the more time is usually required to come to an agreement. Sometimes the group never reaches a consensus. Ultimately, those who have the most persistence or speak the loudest end up "winning" the decision.

On the other hand, if there are fewer than four people involved in the action learning group, it suffers from a number of other equally daunting challenges.

▲ There will be a limited number of perspectives. As a result, the solutions and strategies will not be as creative or innovative as they might be with a larger group.

▲ Too few group members may not allow the group to properly understand and address the complexity of the problem. It will be more difficult to see the many causes of the problem and the possible impact of proposed solutions.

▲ Greater group complexity allows for better systems thinking as a group.

▲ Fewer participants may result in less challenging of one another's basic assumptions and viewpoints.

▲ The group may feel overwhelmed and intimidated by the problem.

▲ The energy of the group may slacken, and excitement may be lost, as one person can easily affect the attitude of the other two members.

▲ There will be less feedback in response to reflective learning questions about individual, team, and organizational growth raised by the action learning coach.

Expectations and Accountability of the Group

In action learning, as will be discussed in greater detail in Chapter 5, the groups are responsible and accountable for developing solid solutions to the problems or tasks assigned to them. The group members' careers, reputations, eventual leadership in the organization, salary increases, and/or future opportunities may well depend on how well they do as a group. Reg Revans called members of action learning groups "comrades in adversity," and others have referred to group members as "fellows in opportunity."

Thus, there is much energy and commitment for members to "hang together" in working through the problem; otherwise they may end up "hanging separately." Even those who may be unfamiliar with the context or have no stake in the outcome will also be accountable and responsible in resolving the problem.

The intensity of working together to successfully develop action strategies is an important component of generating greater learnings as well as building stronger group cohesiveness and supportive behaviors. Of course, the quality of the resulting action is significantly higher when members are accountable for and rewarded for developing great strategies. The fact that the group will also be implementing the action plan enhances the quality of both the learning and the actions.

Action Learning at Fairfax County Public Schools, Virginia

Delores A. Herndon, Career Development Specialist

As part of Fairfax County's leadership program for support employees, an action learning group composed of a maintenance supervisor, two finance assistants, a customer service supervisor, and an administrative assistant was given the challenge of developing a comprehensive orientation program for individuals new to support services. The initial action taken was to survey the various offices in the Human Resources Department to determine the pertinent information needed for new employees. Also, a survey of support employees was taken to determine what information they would like to receive as new employees.

The action learning group developed and submitted to the school district's top leadership a comprehensive orientation program that would be beneficial to all employees, both support and instructional. With great enthusiasm, FCPS incorporated the group's recommendations into what is now the school district's New Employee Orientation program.

Some of the thoughts of participants of the leadership program's action learning groups are as follows:

"Action learning is one of the best tools for solving problems. Different people, ideas, backgrounds, experiences, careers, coming together for one purpose . . . what power."
—Custodial supervisor

"A thinking, open-minded way to share ideas and brainstorm."
—Administrative assistant

"What an outstanding concept. I had fun ironing out team ideas as well as confrontations. I thoroughly enjoyed the experience."
—Maintenance supervisor

"What a great approach to team building and working as a team. My usual [previous] impulse was to get things done and cut off input, thereby reducing ownership of projects."
—Administrative assistant

Importance of Group Diversity

As individuals, we all have mind-sets and assumptions that limit the scope of ideas that we are able to generate. People with different perspectives will challenge our mind-sets and assumptions. Therefore, whenever possible, we should try to balance levels of experience, business unit location, gender, age, and ethnicity to add diversity and richness to action learning groups.

Diversity of group membership contributes immensely to the power and success of action learning, especially when dealing with complex, adaptive problems (see Chapter 2). Weick (1995) notes that teams and organizations need "requisite variety" if they are going to be able to adequately understand and successfully adapt to the complex environment around them. Thus, the more complex the problem, the more important is diverse thinking. Various perspectives provide the opportunity of generating many, rather than just one or two, possible solutions.

Adding the element of reflective inquiry, as we do in action learning, to group diversity multiplies the group's creative powers and magnifies its ability to undertake systems thinking. The wide array of diverse questions forces the group to see problems and challenges with new eyes and in new ways.

We do not see things as they are; we see them as we are.
—The Talmud

Roles of Action Learning Group Members

In action learning programs, there are a number of different roles that involve particular responsibilities. Some of these roles are enacted throughout all the sessions, whereas others may be carried out at the first or last session only or before, between, or after the sessions. Let's look at each of these roles.

Problem Presenter

In a multiple-problem group, each person becomes the presenter for an agreed-upon period of time. In single-problem groups, one person or the entire group may perform the role of problem presenter. There will also be occasions in action learning programs in which the person presenting the problem will be representing the entire business unit or the problem sponsor.

The problem presented should be urgent and significant to the presenter. If the problem comes across as unimportant or trivial, the group will respond accordingly, that is, in a less than energetic and committed fashion. The person should present the problem clearly and concisely. A brief overview is all that is necessary, as the group members will, through their questions, acquire the essential information they need to reframe the problem and begin developing action strategies.

The problem presenter must be willing and must want to be helped. He should believe that the other members really want to assist him in a mutual exploration of problems. He should trust that the group is interested and is able to help. He should also trust the reflective inquiry process of action learning. It is important for the presenter to accept questions with openness and respond clearly and specifically to questions addressed to him. He should avoid answering questions not asked and should not add more detail than has been requested, as this slows down and can sidetrack the group.

It is important that the problem presenter be honest in responding to the questions addressed to him. Of course, there will be questions for which he does not have the answer. There may be others that he needs to reflect on and think about, and there may be some that he does not know how to respond to. And, at any point, he can and should ask questions of the group. Usually, the problem presenter must first feel confident and comfortable in the group before he begins questioning other members. When he does begin questioning, the dynamics of the problem solving changes. Instead of feeling put on the spot, the presenter now senses that the process has become a group opportunity to share and learn. The problem is now transferred from the presenter to the group. The individual's or organization's problem has become the group's problem. Real and effective group problem solving can now begin.

Many of us may find it difficult to ask for help or to answer questions in a way that might indicate some vulnerability on our part. We may feel that it is a flaw or weakness to admit we need help. However, when we come to an action learning session with a problem, we are merely acknowledging that as an individual, business unit, or organization, we are willing to change, to grow, to learn. Only through our acceptance of being vulnerable are we able to capture the ideas and the resources needed to overcome the problem.

It is up to the problem presenter, particularly in multiple-problem sets, to manage the limited time that is available for her. In this way, she is assuming and developing leadership capabilities. By responding clearly, frankly, and reflectively, she enables the group to focus on the key issues and to identify the most powerful actions.

When a person brings a problem to an action learning group, she should be committing to the group not only her willingness to answer questions, but also her commitment to take action between sessions. If the individual or organization does not take the promised action, the group will be less likely to listen and help in later sessions.

At subsequent meetings of the action learning group, the problem presenter will be expected to update the group as to what actions she has taken (or the organization has taken) since the previous meeting, the results of those actions, and the important issues at this point.

Action Learning Coach

The action learning coach is the member of the group who focuses on the learning and development of the group rather than the resolution of the problem. This role may rotate among the group, with a different person serving as the action learning coach at each meeting of the group. Chapter 7 presents more detailed information about the roles and responsibilities of the action learning coach. Suffice it to mention at this point that the main focus of the action learning coach is to help the team to learn and thereby to work better on the problem. Her focus during the sessions remains on the group learning as well as on the application of that learning throughout the organization or in the lives of the individuals.

The action learning coach may have a number of other logistical and orientation responsibilities. She coordinates and manages the sequencing and overall time frame of the action learning sessions. She may also handle administrative issues between sessions. The coach is responsible for orienting the group at its first meeting regarding the purposes and principles of action learning and the role of the action learning coach. She might serve as the link to top management, to the sponsor, and to the champion (of the problem). In some organizations, she may also be the action learning champion.

Members of the Action Learning Group

The members of the action learning group may have voluntarily joined, or may have been appointed to, the group to help solve the problem(s) submitted to the group; to develop specific leadership, team, or individual skills; or to generate better collaboration among departments, between staff and customers, or among other units. The primary responsibility of each group member, including the problem presenter, is to ask questions and to respond to those questions addressed to him or her specifically or to those questions addressed to the group at large.

Group members should ask questions that are helpful to the problem, rather than questions that serve one's own purposes (such as gaining information for oneself or making oneself look knowledgeable). The focus is on the questions rather than on one's opinions. Group members should allow adequate time for everyone to ask questions. Sometimes individuals need to delay their own questions to allow active participation by all.

Individual members should remember that they do not have to solve the problem; they will be doing their job, and doing it well, if they just ask great questions. The questioning process will solve the problem. It is valuable for group members to recognize that periods of silence can be liberating to all members, especially the problem presenter, who may sometimes feel overwhelmed by the questioning.

Group members should be willing to try new ways of doing things, to experiment, to take risks, to ask questions, and to reflect on their experiences. They should be active by word and by body language in supporting their fellow learners. Members should provide colleagues with genuine support, encouragement, and assistance and cultivate an attitude of empathy. Individuals build strong groups by listening to each other's questions and asking questions that show they have listened and thus care. The more people build trust, the more group members will feel comfortable taking risks.

When an individual becomes a member of an action learning group, it is important for that person to be present at every meeting and stay for the entire meeting. The powerful cohesiveness of an action learning group is unlike any other type of group. When someone is absent, a valuable element is lost. Teamwork, and especially team thinking and team learning, requires participation by all members.

When the group has reached a consensus on the true and important problem, the group members should ask questions that generate action plans and action points. It is important not to jump prematurely into solutions (usually the action learning coach will ask questions to confirm agreement before moving forward). Group members should avoid becoming impatient or defensive at such junctures.

Group members should be enthusiastic about the opportunities to learn, rather than frustrated that the time for learning seems to be taking time away from the urgent problem. They should pride themselves on being able to ask fresh questions and thereby contribute richness to resolving the problem. Individuals should bring forth their unique perspectives while at the same time examining their own assumptions and quality of participation. Everyone has the ability to contribute to forming an environment of mutual support in which there is rich dialogue that leads to great solutions and learnings.

At the end of each session, action steps will be identified, which may involve gathering information, testing a plan, or seeking resources or support. Group members are held accountable for carrying out actions that they commit to undertake.

Problem Sponsor

An organizational problem generally has a sponsor who may or may not be a member of the group. The sponsor is someone who understands the nature of the problem, thinks it is important, and can be influential in helping the group gain access to necessary resources. The sponsor appoints himself or someone else to be present in the group. He makes certain that the problem is given high visibility and acceptance and ensures that the organization will be committed to taking action.

If the problem sponsor is not able to be present in the group, she should make every effort to appear before the group at the first meeting to provide a brief background of the problem and answer questions raised by the action learning group before departing. There may be subsequent sessions in which she will be asked to appear again to answer more questions about the problem or to provide feedback relative to the strategies and actions being considered. It is important to note that a problem sponsor who is not a permanent member of the group should be there only to respond to questions, and not to assert her authority or prejudge the work of the group, unless the group asks for her thoughts or judgments.

Organization's Action Learning Champion

Normally, the organization's action learning champion does not participate in the group meetings. However, there may be occasions when the action learning group determines that it needs information or special support and assistance from this person. Accordingly, the group may request his presence at an action learning session to respond to inquiries of the group. However, the major role and service that the champion provides to the group is to assure them of the company's overall commitment to action learning.

Action Learning Members: Volunteers or Volunteered?

Action learning groups may be composed of volunteers, appointees of the organization, or some combination of the two. Depending on the specific goals of the action learning program, companies may request volunteers or appoint particular individuals to join the action learning group(s). For example, if there is a companywide initiative and corporate strategy to create a corporatewide culture, a cross section of staff members may be chosen to form the groups. If the issue is more focused, such as creating a new staff appraisal system, participants may either be selected according to interest and/or knowledge or be allowed to volunteer.

Individuals may volunteer to belong to an action learning group for a variety of reasons: because of their interest in the topic, their desire to work with this particular group of individuals, their wish to be recognized by top management as being committed to action learning, and/or their commitment to learn, practice, and develop new leadership and team capabilities and skills. Whether members are "volunteered" by the organization or volunteer themselves, it is important for action learning programs to avoid creating groups in which members form a clique or tend to think alike or simply enjoy being together. Such situations may provide ease and comfort to the members, but will probably result in limited innovation and breakthrough thinking.

Intactness of Group and Use of Outside Resources

In action learning groups, the intense learnings, deep sharing of personal perspectives, critical responsibility, and direct accountability all place high expectations on the group. The high level of teamwork that is created via the reflective inquiry process and the interventions of the coach create an important group solidarity. Once the membership of the group has been established, it should stay intact throughout its existence. Putnam (2000) notes that the most complex problems can be solved only by a group that has developed a strong social bonding. Therefore, it is much better that the group meet fewer times when everyone is present than more times when one or more of the members may be absent.

There may be occasions when an outsider is invited to join the group as a resource to respond to questions raised by the group. Outsiders might thus attend parts of a particular session or sessions. They should be invited when the group as a whole determines that they can be of help in providing information or support relative to the resolution of the problem. Usually action learning groups will need to interact with outside people between action learning sessions as they seek information, identify resources, and test action strategies.

**The Pizza Man Delivers Fresh
Questions Worth $35 Million**

An engineering consulting firm, commissioned to develop an innovative, cost-cutting process for a government department, quickly established a task force to work on the problem. The team leader, Bill, introduced the group to action learning and encouraged the engineers and scientists to use this approach. Progress, however, was slow and new breakthrough ideas were not emerging. And the final project was due within a week.

One day, as the group was working late into the evening, they decided to order out for pizza so they could continue wrestling with the project for a couple more hours. When the pizza man arrived, Bill made a startling request. Noting that his group was composed only of internal engineers who had similar experiences and viewpoints, he decided that a different, fresh perspective was needed. "How about joining us for the next hour and earning a big tip?" he asked the pizza man. "We will check with your boss and get his approval. All you need to do is listen to what we are doing. If there is anything that you do not understand or you see wall charts that don't make sense to you, all you have to do is ask questions." This sounded good to the pizza man, although one can imagine the surprise and frustration felt by Bill's colleagues, who probably muttered, "We have only a couple more days to work on this project, and now we are going to waste an hour with a pizza man!?"

The pizza man sat down. After several minutes of listening and observing, he decided he would have to earn his tip. He noticed a chart on the wall and asked why an arrow went from point A to point F. A disgruntled group member gave a reason, but then another member said, "No, there is another, better reason." A third member chimed in, "Well, if the second reason is okay, why don't we simply go from point A to point D?" The group realized that the pizza man's "dumb" question had caused them to examine some unchallenged assumptions they all had been making.

After the pizza man left, the group began with clean sheets of paper and a determination to look outside the box. Over the next couple days, they incorporated many new ideas that emerged from the fresh questions of the pizza man. Their breakthrough project was submitted to the government, which resulted in a $35 million savings over the life of the contract. Thanks to the pizza man! ■

Action Learning Engages All Types of Personalities

Because of the inquisitive and reflective nature of action learning groups as well as their commitment to thinking and acting, all types of personalities can actively and effectively participate. Both introverts and extroverts, for example, can excel in the action learning process, because the focus on questions levels the playing field. Those individuals who are quiet by nature are given the time and encouragement to verbalize their insights and ideas, so instead of sitting back and becoming frustrated by the outgoing personalities, they can more easily express themselves and contribute to the work of the group. On the other hand, the reflective inquiry process slows down the extroverts, enabling them to listen better and contribute with more reflective substance.

Action learning needs and assists the participation of reflective types as well as action-oriented individuals. Reflectors are critical, as they tend to raise questions more easily than the action-oriented people, who, on the other hand, will prevent the group from reaching "analysis paralysis." Pragmatists will emphasize the details and follow-up actions, while the theorists are valuable in seeking new solutions that are broad and systemic. Action learning requires and encourages both types; the group examines the present and what is working or not working but also is forced to seek innovative, untried systems-changing solutions. Those who need quick solutions are forced to ensure that the problem has been properly reframed and that the solutions will achieve the goal and not create other problems. This reassures those who feel constricted by structure and deadlines that decisions are not moving too fast. Action learning is not only concerned with strategic, logical solutions (which appeal to the rational, thinking types), but also with the quality of interaction and the growth and learning of the group and individuals (which appeals to the more feeling-based types).

Success with Groups at Baxter International

Baxter International, an $8 billion global pharmaceutical market leader, recently began a large-scale Leadership for Growth Action Learning Program. Baxter's action learning groups were composed of high-potential vice presidents selected by Human Resources, additional vice presidents, and top business unit leaders. Each group had coaches, sponsors, and team members.

Baxter International saw the action learning program as an opportunity to develop a number of skills relative to business issues (e.g., strategic thinking, business knowledge, and customer insight) and leadership competencies (self-awareness, team leadership, and change leadership). Baxter's experience with action learning resulted in a number of valuable lessons. First, the organization realized the value and importance of action learning coaches, not only during the sessions but also between sessions, when they also provided coaching assistance to the participants. The focus on learning and development as well as resolving problems also made the action learning extremely valuable. The organization also recognized the importance of wisely selecting who would be in the action learning groups and discovered that continuous feedback should be provided to the group members. Executive sponsorship proved to be important in implementing the following:

▲ Defining the business issue scope and deliverables with the team
▲ Providing political support
▲ Keeping top management informed about progress
▲ Monitoring the action plans of the action learning groups
▲ Ensuring follow-up on project decisions ■

Precautions with Subject-Matter Experts

One of the ways in which action learning differs from most problem-solving groups is that action learning deliberately seeks group members who possess different perspectives rather than filling the group with individuals who possess expertise on the problem or the context. Research shows that solving complex problems demands diversity more than it requires expertise.

Experts can be detrimental to the success of problem-solving groups for a number of reasons. Although experts can provide valuable information, they can also think too much within the box—the natural tendency when one has become highly specialized in a subject area. With their superior knowledge, experts will tend to dominate the group's discussions. Those with less expertise, in turn, will become uncomfortable in making statements or even raising questions they fear will be perceived as "dumb" by the experts. The nonexperts may also hesitate to offer solutions, fearing them to be ideas that the experts may have long ago discarded.

Experts also create dependence and/or risk avoidance on the part of the other group members. We are all aware of the disasters that have occurred when only experts dominated the decision making and there was an absence of fresh questions from the nonexperts. Catastrophes such as the sinking of the *Titanic* and the failure of the *Challenger* shuttle have been attributed to the inability of nonexperts to challenge the experts in their groups. Experts can immobilize group members as well as decrease the development of individual and group confidence.

Thus, expertise in confronting problems is more valuable than expertise with the answers. Freedom to consider new ideas is essential if groups are to be innovative when working on problems and seeking fresh solutions. A key advantage of the action learning group is its ability to interpret or make sense of confusing information instead of having a scientific and easy answer.

Lockheed Martin's Virtual Action Learning Groups

Action learning groups at Lockheed Martin were composed of leaders from throughout the United States. As a result, members could only occasionally meet at the same physical site. Lockheed Martin was very pleased with the successes of the groups. To further develop the capability of future action learning groups that would need to meet virtually, the groups reflected on the following questions at their final session:

▲ What successes did you have while working virtually?
▲ What factors contributed to these?
▲ What were you not able to do?
▲ How are virtual teams different from physically intact teams?
▲ What are some learnings for future work in virtual teams?   ■

Virtual Action Learning Groups

As more and more groups are required to work in virtual situations, many organizations are exploring the possibility of creating virtual action learning teams. Research shows that virtual groups, who share an interest but not the same space, can be more egalitarian, frank, and task oriented than groups that communicate face-to-face (Putnam, 2000). However, teams that work virtually rather than in person encounter a number of significant challenges.

Because of the paucity of social cues and communication, computer-based groups will find it harder to reach consensus and will feel less solidarity with one another. When we meet face-to-face, we are effective at sensing nonverbal messages from one another, especially about emotions, cooperation, and trustworthiness. We lose that ability when we cannot see the other people with whom we are interacting. In addition, virtual groups often develop a sense of depersonalization and are less satisfied with the group's accomplishments.

Although computer-based groups are quicker to reach an intellectual understanding of their shared problems, they are much worse at generating the trust and reciprocity necessary to implement that understanding (Putnam, 2000). In issues and situations that are clear and practical, virtual groups can function reasonably well. However, more serious difficulties and frustrations occur in situations of uncertainty and heavy accountability.

How can we develop the technology and adapt action learning to enhance social presence, feedback, and behavioral cues necessary for successful group problem solving? Virtual action learning, like face-to-face action learning, requires the competent intervention of the action learning coach. The coach should supplement the power and value of technology with her reflective questions to better enable the participants to share cues and feedback. As the group members gain comfort and confidence with the computer-mediated meeting, the coach can assist the group in reflecting about what is being learned and how the learning is occurring.

With end-user software becoming increasingly less difficult to navigate, action learning participants can more easily share both cognitive knowledge and social cues. As software developers build new e-commerce applications, action learning should be incorporated into the design so that these new applications can complement the elements of action learning.

Yoong and Gallupe (2001), Bannan-Ritland (2001), and other researchers continue to search for ways in which action learning principles can be applied to virtual work groups. A growing number of organizations, such as the U.S. Department of Agriculture and George Washington University, are using virtual action learning teams with increasing levels of success.

Virtual Action Learning at George Washington University

Six students in my action learning course at George Washington University participated in a virtual multiple-problem action learning set. On Wednesday evenings for six weeks, they each took a turn presenting a problem/task they faced. Capitalizing on chat and other online technologies, they asked questions and reflected on proposed strategies. The group rotated the role of the action learning coach. The group reported great success in that each individual was helped, and the team learned about leadership, groups, and themselves. ∎

Cooperative Work Groups Are More Successful

Members in action learning teams seek to work in a highly cooperative and collaborative manner. The six components and two ground rules initiate and sustain the needed supportive and positive behaviors. Johnson and Johnson (1989), in their research on hundreds of work groups, concluded that cooperative work groups are much more successful than work groups in which members compete with one another. Their analysis identified four major advantages for cooperative work groups:

▲ Work groups that had collaborative norms and behavior had greater productivity.

▲ Such groups demonstrated a higher quality of reasoning strategies. Reasoning strategies include the ability of the group to integrate new information with prior knowledge, to identify concepts underlying data, to problem solve, to implement metaphoric reasoning, and to increase metacognition. Metacognition is critical for groups because it leads to the generalized improvement in learning capability.

▲ There is a better quality of work relations in cooperative work groups. New ideas and solutions are generated, which would not have occurred if individuals were working independently.

▲ Finally, in cooperative work groups, there is wider and better transfer of learning. With more complex understandings, cooperative situations produce greater transfer of the learnings back to the organization.

Characteristics of Effective Action Learning Groups

High-performance work groups exhibit a number of common characteristics that initiate and sustain their success. The principles, components, ground rules, and activities of action learning synergistically generate and reinforce the following key attributes of successful work teams.

A Shared Commitment to Solving the Problem

A critical ingredient for successful groups is the members' commitment to the work of the group. In action learning, the group has been brought together for the purpose of solving a single problem or problems that are important to one or all of the members. Group members realize that they must work together to succeed and, if successful, they will be rewarded as a group. An added dimension occurs with multiple problem sets in that everyone helps each other with his or her specific problems; thus, there is a feeling that since you have helped me with my problem, I will make an effort and commitment to helping you to solve your problem.

Revans and the Mines of Wales and England

Reg Revans's first job was HR director for mines in Wales and England. His first challenge was to increase the low productivity in the mines as well as to raise the low morale of the mine workers. Instead of seeking outside expertise,

Reg decided to ask the miners themselves what could be done. The miners, of course, had lots of ideas. They were in the mines every day and saw things that worked and things that were just outright stupid. The miners were also strongly committed to identifying solutions that would increase safety as well as production, since they would need to return to the mines after their solutions had been implemented (unlike the consultants who did not have to go down into the mines to see if their solutions were viable). The miners clearly had a common and strong commitment to solving the problems. As a result, the mines where Reg worked had productivity levels 30 percent above the other mines of Wales and England, and not surprisingly, morale was much higher. ■

Clear, Common Purpose

Members of most groups assume that they all have a clear and common understanding and agreement as to their group's purpose. However, when they are asked to state what it is, there is invariably a wide array of opinions. Even when a specific goal is presented to us at the same time and in the same location, each of us hears it differently. Why? Because our backgrounds and experiences cause us to interpret concepts quite differently. Thus, although we may think we are trying to accomplish the same thing, in reality, we are often working at cross-purposes with our fellow group members. Therefore, an absolutely critical component for any group to maintain short-term and long-term success is for it to reach a consensus as to its purpose. In action learning, we never assume that there is agreement on what the group is expected to do. Action learning groups begin by clarifying the goal and achieving consensus on it. Research shows that consensus on a goal is possible only when the group members ask questions about the goal and each other's understanding of the goal. To confirm the consensus, the action learning coach checks with the group regularly before allowing group members to begin working on solutions. Most groups jump in quickly, trying to reach agreement on strategies when they do not have agreement on the goal, and thus many hours or days may be spent by members trying to force one another to accept their strategy. It is very difficult, however, to agree on strategy if we are striving for different goals. It is much easier to agree on strategies if everyone agrees on the goal.

Willingness to Work with Others to Develop Strategies

High-performing groups require members who are willing, committed, and even excited about working together. Action learning begins with a complex problem, one in which there is no known solution and a variety of options are possible. No one has all the information or resources or political power to resolve it. Thus the perspectives, knowledge, and experience of all group members are necessary. Members need each other's help to think through the ideas and to pilot test them. In action learning groups, the members may have been thrust into problems and situations entirely new to them as the organization seeks individuals with fresh questions as well as individuals who have experience with the issue. Effective work groups must have members who are open to new ideas, who recognize that people with different perspectives will see things they don't see.

Courage to Question Others

For a group to be effective, its members must be able and willing to question each other, to challenge ideas and statements, no matter who the other members may be. In action learning, everyone is expected, even required, to ask questions of each other and the group. Consequently, members quickly develop the ability and confidence to ask questions, and they soon see the immense value of the questioning process. Many members also enjoy the fact that focusing on questions removes the burden of having to have all the answers. Although it may in fact be difficult to ask good questions, most people soon realize that questioning is easier than having answers, and they jump into reflective inquiry with greater gusto and openness than they initially imagined they would.

Clear and Accepted Norms

High-performing groups need to have clear norms, whether they are imposed on the group or have been built by and agreed to by all the members. All action learning groups begin with the norms contained in the six components and two ground rules, namely, reflective inquiry, questions before statements, commitment to learning, confidentiality, focusing on problem solving and taking action, and the power of the action learning coach. Each group then establishes additional norms during the first intervention of the action learning coach when she asks the following questions: "How are we doing thus far as a group? What are we doing well? What could we do better?"

As each action learning group responds to these questions, its members are consciously and subconsciously establishing the norms that they will be adhering to during the rest of their time together. For

Table 2	*Stages of Group Life*

Typical Groups	Action Learning Groups
Forming	Forming
Storming	Performing
Norming	Norming
Performing	Performing

example, if a member of the group says, "We have been listening well," the coach will ask for examples as well as the reasons the group members may have been listening well. This discussion imprints itself on the psyche and behavior of the group members. The group invariably continues to behave in the manner it has determined to be "good behavior." After responding to "What could be improved?" the group immediately begins to behave in the ways that it has suggested. Norms, therefore, are actually set as the group focuses on its responses to the questions. These norms are always positive, for example, listening, respecting, being creative, questioning, reflecting, committing, and so forth. Amazingly, these norms are so powerfully ingrained through the reflective discussions that it is very difficult for an individual member to step outside these group-created norms, and norms are thus rarely violated.

Why Action Learning Groups Can Skip Storming

A remarkable characteristic of action learning groups is that, as a result of the coach's intervention (see Chapter 7) and the action-reflection orientation, these groups go through different stages than other problem-solving groups. Instead of the typical path of forming, storming, norming, and performing, action learning groups go immediately from forming to performing (working on a specific problem), then to norming (with the action learning coach's "what is working and what can be done better" questions), and then back to performing, thereby skipping the stage of storming altogether (see Table 2). Many problem-solving groups have such a difficult storming phase that they never fully recover from the pain they inflicted on one another and, as a result, never perform very well. Members never truly enjoy being part of such groups. Action learning groups, on the other hand, are filled with fulfilling and enjoyable experiences. ∎

Respect and Support for Others

Successful work groups are filled with members who are respectful of each other and interested to learn about others' perspectives and viewpoints. As a result of the interplay of the six components of action learning, particularly as members share their learnings and vulnerabilities through the interventions of the action learning coach, action learning members generate a positive and healthy self-regard for one another. In one group in which I served as the action learning coach, two of the participants had worked together for more than fifteen years, could not tolerate each other, and certainly did not respect the talent or efforts of the other. Yet, amazingly, within sixty minutes of working together in an action learning group, they were questioning and listening to each other, sharing and respecting each other's ideas and strategies. After the session ended, one commented, "This is the first time in fifteen years that I really felt able to work with him, that he really had some commitment to our organization and wanted to contribute."

Willingness to Learn and to Help Others Learn

Successful groups need to have members who are willing to learn and develop themselves as well as help the members around them to learn and develop their competencies. When people join an action learning group, they are clearly informed that the group has two purposes: to work on the issue and to learn. They know that time and energy will be spent on developing individual and team capacities. Accepting the need to learn and help others learn engenders a helping, sharing attitude as well as a sense of humility among the group members. Such attitudes build not only powerful, but also sensitive and caring groups.

Cohesiveness and Trust

Action learning group members are tightly connected to each other as they work out the problem. As they jointly focus on reframing the problem and developing strategies, they are also building strong bonds. Interconnectedness is also built by the egalitarian nature of action learning groups, in which the quality of questions rather than the ability to provide answers is important. Finally, high levels of trust are built when people share their vulnerabilities, that is, that they have problems and they need to learn. As a result, action learning groups are energizing and enjoyable for the participants.

Checklist for Action Learning Group Membership

▲ What are the criteria for membership in the action learning group?

▲ Are the group members from diverse backgrounds and ethnicities?

▲ Are members here by choice or by appointment?

▲ Is the size of groups between four and eight members?

▲ Will the groups operate full time or part time?

▲ Is there a balance between experts and nonexperts? Individuals familiar and unfamiliar with the problem and the context?

▲ Do we have members from outside the organization—customers, suppliers, dealers, other organizations?

▲ What is the level of accountability and responsibility for the group's results?

▲ Are all members committed to be present at all the meetings?

▲ Is there a sense of ownership of the problem?

▲ What access to outside resource people will be available?

▲ Are the dates and times established?

▲ Will any groups be meeting virtually?

CHAPTER

4

Questions and Reflection

Questions serve many purposes for action learning groups. They enable members to understand, to clarify, and to open up new avenues of exploration for solving the problem. They provide new insights and ideas for strategic actions and potential paths for solutions. Questions build understandings while laying the groundwork for gaining support for possible actions. Questions also serve as the foundation for individual, team, and organizational learning.

The important thing is not to stop questioning.
—Albert Einstein

One of the primary ways in which action learning differs from other problem-solving approaches is by focusing on questions rather than on solutions. Only through questions can a group truly gain a common understanding of the problem, acquire a sense of each other's potential strategies, and achieve innovative, breakthrough strategies and solutions. Questions, when asked at the right time in the right way, provide the glue that holds the group together. The seeds of the answer are con-

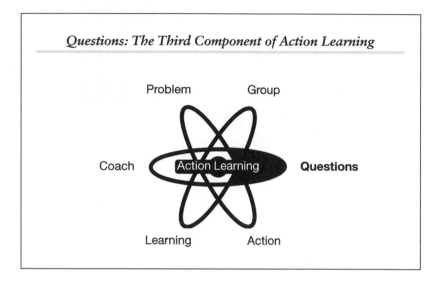

Questions: The Third Component of Action Learning

tained in the kernel of the questions. Thus, the better the questions, the better will be the solutions as well as the learnings; the deeper the reflection, the greater the development of individual and team competencies.

Action learning recognizes that problem solving must begin by first diverging, through the use of inquiry, and only then should the narrowing and converging occur. First the group must gain the big picture of the problem, see the "entire elephant," before determining possible goals and specific strategies. The acquisition of a wide, helicopter view of the problem can be accomplished only by openly and freshly questioning each other and then reflecting on the responses. A central aspect of action learning is the reflective inquiry process and the resulting group environment that allows for and encourages people to ask "dumb" or, more accurately, "fresh" questions.

Seven Blind Men and the Elephant

A well-known Hindu fable tells the story of the seven blind men who encounter an elephant for the first time. The man who felt the ear said, "This is a large leaf." The man who grabbed a leg said, "No, this is a tree trunk." The man who felt the tail said, "It is a thick rope," and the man who touched the elephant's flank declared it to be a wall. "No, it is a snake," said the man who touched the trunk. The sixth man said it was a bag as he felt the elephant's mouth. Touching the tusk, the seventh man declared that it was a spear. ■

The obvious, but not always practiced, first step in solving any problem is to be sure you know what the problem is. Most of us assume, because we heard about or experienced the problem, that we now know and understand exactly what the problem is. And, what is more dangerous, we believe everyone else now has the same perception and understanding of the problem. The reality is that seven people who hear about or even experience the same problem, in fact, discern it and describe it quite differently. Why? Because we all, like the seven blind men, come to the reality with different perspectives, perspectives created by our previous experiences as well as our diverse ages, genders, cultures, and other social and educational backgrounds.

For action learning proponents, these differences, although causing some initial challenges, are positive and valuable for problem solving and strategy development. Why? Because problems by their nature are complex and complicated, and proposed solutions can affect the environment in innumerable ways. Different perspectives and the resulting fresh questions are necessary to fully understand the problem (e.g., that it is an elephant), and only when there is agreement that it is indeed an elephant, can workable strategies (e.g., pulling the trunk) emerge that will enable us to move the elephant.

Power of Questions

Questions will always be more powerful than statements in solving problems and developing concerted actions. The key to the power of action learning resides in the quality and flow of questions. Accordingly, action learning places a high priority on group members asking good, challenging questions. Asking the right question is not an easy task, especially when the group is struggling with an overwhelming problem (fighting the alligators). Revans (1982a) notes, "The capacity to ask fresh questions in conditions of ignorance, risk, and confusion, when nobody knows what to do next" is at the heart of action learning. John Morris (1991), a leading pioneer in action learning, remarks that only "through constant questioning do we see more clearly just who we really are, and what remarkable resources we have access to. We will also see more clearly what is really facing us, and we will become more capable of accepting and responding to change."

In action learning, we focus on the right questions rather than on the right answers, because we know that the right questions will lead us to the right answer and that the beginnings to the answer will lie in the questions. Questions help the group to recognize and reorganize their knowledge. As group members are engaged in asking questions of each other, they gradually gain a group consensus on answers and strategies, since they now more clearly see each others' perspectives and have greater clarity on their own.

Questions, especially challenging ones, cause us to think and to learn. Questions create energy and vitality in the group, since they trigger a need to listen, to seek a common truth, and to justify opinions and viewpoints. Questions generate a dialogue in which people begin to leave their individual limitations to find a new wholeness.

An interesting phenomenon occurs as we ask questions about someone else's problem. The questioning process causes us to become more interested in the problem. And when we listen to someone respond to our question, we appreciate their efforts and their attention. Group members will find the truth more easily through listening to each other's questions and reflections than by being forced to listen to opinions and statements that are based on assumptions. Truth does not emerge from opinions but from the free movement of open minds. Questioning causes us to view each other as learning resources.

The Titanic, the Bay of Pigs, and the Challenger

What do the sinking of the *Titanic,* the Bay of Pigs incident, and the *Challenger* disaster have in common? According to historians who have carefully examined the background and details of these three events, the common element was the inability or unwillingness of participants to raise questions about their concerns. Some group members were fearful that they were the only one who had a particular concern (when, in fact, it was later discovered that many people in the group had similar concerns). Others felt that their question had already been answered in the mind of the group; if they asked, it would be considered a dumb question. But because individuals did not ask questions, lives were lost in each of these tragedies. Thus, an important tenet of action learning is to create a structure and environment in which people are encouraged to ask what they might think of as "dumb" questions. Often it is the "dumb" question that is really the great "fresh" question that ultimately solves the problem and perhaps saves the company. ■

Benefits of Questions

Questions provide four powerful benefits to the action learning process, namely, problem solving, team building, leadership development, and learning enhancement. Let's examine each of these.

Problem Solving

In action learning, questions are asked not just to seek answers, but to understand, to respond to what is being asked, to force us to think. The focus is not on a quest for solutions only, but also to generate opportunities to explore and to learn. For purposes of problem exploration and solving, research shows that questions are always more powerful than statements in clarifying, in gaining mutual agreement, and in gaining a consensus of perspective (Cooperrider, Sorensen, and Yaeger, 2001; Marsick, 1992). Questioning forces us to listen carefully in order to stay in the game.

Questions and reflection allow time for the minds of all the members to be working. This simultaneous learning, a type of "team thinking," is much faster than talking, especially talking that is interrupted by more talking. Being responsible for asking good questions takes the burden off individuals to solve the problem. No one needs to be defensive or take sole responsibility for finding the answers.

Responding to questions enables the group to become aware of inconsistencies as well as consistencies. Responding to questions causes the problem presenter to "talk out loud" his thoughts, thereby creating clarity and insights not possible when he contains the process in his own mind. Weick (1995) describes the process as constructive insight, or "How can I know what I'm thinking until I hear what I've said?"

Team Building

Questions build strong and cohesive teams because of the many positive effects they have on a group of people. Questions require us to listen to other people and can affect how we feel toward other group members. For example, we tend to reconstruct how we perceive and value someone who is asking us for our knowledge and opinions. Questions tend to make the person being questioned feel important. We think, "Maybe the person asking me questions is smart, since he recognizes my intelligence and values my perspectives."

When everyone is expected to focus on questioning and the primary form of communication is questions, it is very difficult, if not impossible, for one person to dominate the discussion. People can participate in the interactions only through the asking of questions or the answering of someone else's question. If the question posed is not useful, the group may move on to another person's inquiry.

Questions also have the power to build strong group cohesion. Inquiries go to the center of the table, and the focus is on the question rather than on the person asking or answering the question. Synergy and togetherness grow as people work on what has now become the group's question, as members develop group solutions. When the group develops innovative insights and solutions as a result of the questions, ever stronger bonds and support are generated. Questions, by their very nature, also cause individuals and teams to be more receptive to adapting, changing, and growing.

Leadership Development

What is the most important skill of a leader? Vaill (1996), Senge (1990), and many other management theorists, as well as CEOs such as Ollila (Nokia), Gates (Microsoft), and Chambers (Cisco Systems), cite the ability to ask great questions. Throughout history, from Socrates to Senge, asking the right question has been seen as a mark of the wise man. Kotter (1998), a noted Harvard University business professor, stated that the primary difference between a leader and a manager is that leaders are those who can ask the right questions, and managers are those tasked to answer them. Asking the right questions enables us to discover the right response, and the right response enables us to take the right action.

In action learning, everyone receives ample time to practice and demonstrate the art of asking questions. With the guidance of the action learning coach, the group reflects on the quality and impact of the group's questions. In action learning, we believe that finding the right question is more important than answering well the wrong question.

Questions require us to listen carefully and reflect. They demonstrate our ability to empathize and care about others. Questions can motivate as much or more than exhortatory statements. Finally, questions cause us and the people around us to think, to learn, and to grow.

Learning Enhancement

Education theorists (Bruner, 1974; Bandura, 1977; Knowles, Holton, and Swanson, 1998) note that deep and significant learning occurs only as a result of reflection, and reflection is not possible without a question—whether the question is from an external source or from within one's own mind. Thus the central action learning process of reflective inquiry presents the perfect way to optimize individual and team learning.

Questions have a physiological impact on the synapses of our brain. The synapses open wider and make more connections because of the body's need to deal with the question. To demonstrate this, take a heading in this or any book and convert it into a question. For example, look at the statement "Action learning helps us to learn." If you simply ask yourself, "How does action learning help us to learn?" you will be surprised at how much more you will learn and retain of what you read in that section.

In action learning we learn not only about what directly causes the problem or what solution may work (which is single-loop learning), but we also seek to discover and learn what might be the underlying causes and solutions (double-loop learning) as well as the culture and the mind-set that create these causes and solutions (triple-loop learning).

A final way in which action learning helps people to learn is through the supportive, creative environment of the group. When people respond in a positive way to the questions you ask (as occurs frequently), it gives you confidence, a feeling of self-worth and importance, and an appreciation of the learning environment, all of which contribute to your learning mentality and success.

When in an epoch of change, when tomorrow is necessarily different from yesterday, new ways of thinking must emerge. New questions need to be asked before solutions are sought. Action learning's primary objective is to learn how to ask appropriate questions under conditions of risk rather than find answers to questions that have already been defined by others. We have to act ourselves into a new way of thinking rather than think ourselves into a new way of acting.
—Reg Revans

Make Statements Only in Response to Questions

This is the first ground rule of action learning. Questions are at the heart of action learning and contribute immensely to the success of action learning. As we have discussed, much of the potency of action learning is built upon questions that generate reflective inquiry. Because questions are so important and powerful in solving problems, generating learning, and building leaders and teams, it is critical to ensure that questions rather than statements are the primary means of communication in action learning. Therefore, we strongly encourage action learning groups and the action learning coach to establish this ground rule: *Statements can be made only in response to questions.*

This ground rule does not prohibit the use of statements; as a matter of fact, there may still be more statements than questions during the action learning meetings since every question asked may generate one or more responses from each of the other members of the group, or up to five to ten statements per question.

Requiring people to think "questions first" transforms the dynamics of the group. The natural impulse to make statements and judgments must give way to listening and reflecting. Once the problem or task has been introduced to the group, the members must first ask questions to clarify the problem before jumping into statements to solve the problem. In action learning, we recognize that there is a correlation between the number and quality of questions and the quality of the resulting actions and learnings. Balancing the number of questions and the number of statements leads to dialogue, which is a proper balance between advocating and inquiring.

This ground rule provides tremendous value to the action learning group. First, it forces everyone in the group to think about asking questions, about inquiring rather than making statements or advocating. Questions tend to unite; statements can cause divisions. An environment in which questions are valued requires people to listen to each other. Questions prevent domination by a single person and instead create cohesion.

Does this ground rule limit the free flow of interaction among group members? It may slow down the rapid flow of communication, but in action learning this is seen as positive, as it forces members to be reflective and creative, to listen first.

Will some people manipulate this rule, raising their voices at the end of statements to convert them to questions? This is certainly possible, but once any statement is converted into a question, the power then moves to the respondents, who may choose to agree or not agree, to reflect upon the question or to respond with a more open question.

It is amazing how quickly group members become comfortable and competent in this approach to communications. As action learning groups experience the tremendous benefits of questioning, they gladly embrace this precept. It recaptures their natural way of communicating and learning as young children before the impulse was inhibited by adults telling them to "stop asking so many questions." The quality of the group's work and the comfort of the interactions often cause members to apply this ground rule in other parts of organizational life.

Questions Enhance and Advance Knowledge

In most problem-solving situations, only the knowledge that is brought into the group by its members is utilized. This knowledge (which action learning refers to as programmed knowledge, or "P") allows for an incremental, narrowly focused understanding and mediocre solution to the problem but rarely generates the quantum improvements or spectacular leaps in knowledge necessary to solve today's more complex problems. Programmed knowledge alone is simply unable to solve problems from a systems perspective.

Only through questions and reflection (that is, the reflective inquiry process of action learning) can a group generate a holistic broad-based perspective. By seeing each other as learners and learning resources, members of an action learning group anticipate the generation of new knowledge within the group. Questioning builds on the knowledge that people bring into the group while at the same time constructing new knowledge and learning.

By beginning with questioning rather than using past knowledge as the reference point, the group can gauge whether the present available information is adequate and relevant to the situation. The key to problem solving is to start with fresh questions, not constructs and assumptions from the past. Questions enable groups to unpeel the layers around the problem and uncover the core elements of knowledge necessary to discover the solution.

Types of Questions in Action Learning

There are several types of questions that can be asked in action learning sessions, all of which build the group's capacity to understand and reframe the problem, to build common goals, to develop potential strategies, and to take effective actions. Questions not only build a deeper and better understanding of the problem and possible solutions, but also construct better working relations among the problem solvers Here are some examples of questions that members should be encouraged to utilize in action learning sessions.

> *Open questions.* These are questions that give the person or group a high degree of freedom in deciding how to respond; for example, "What would be the best results if we took that action?"

> *Affective questions.* Such questions invite members to share feelings about an issue: "How do you feel about leaving this job?"

Reflective questions. These encourage more elaboration; for example, "You said there are difficulties with your manager; what do you think causes these difficulties?"

Probing questions. These questions cause the person or group to go into more depth or breadth on a topic: "Why is this happening?"

Fresh questions. Such questions challenge basic assumptions; for example, "Why must it be that way?" "What do you always . . . ?" "Has this ever been tried?"

Questions that create connections. These help to create a systems perspective; for example, "What are the consequences of these actions?"

Clarifying questions. These are questions that result in further descriptions and explanations, such as, "Are you saying that . . . ?" "Could you explain more about this situation?"

Explorative questions. These open up new avenues and insights and lead to new explorations: "Have you explored/thought of . . . ?" "Would such a source help?"

Analytical questions. Such questions examine causes and not just symptoms; for example, "Why has this happened?"

Closed questions. These can be answered by "yes" or "no," or a quantitative response can be useful to clarify or seek further understanding and quickly move the group forward; for example, "How many people will be affected?" "Did you agree with this decision?"

The types of questions that are not helpful in action learning are *leading questions,* those that force or encourage the person or group to respond in the way intended by the questioner (for example, "You wanted to do it by yourself, didn't you?"), and *multiple questions,* a string of questions put together to meet the needs of the questioner but confusing to the responder.

The attitude in which questions are asked is very important in action learning. Questions should be asked for the purpose of enabling the group members to broaden and deepen their view of the situation or issue they are addressing. Thus it is important that the set members adjust their style from that of eliciting/interrogating to that of enabling (McGill and Beaty, 1995).

You look at what's there and say, Why? I dream about what isn't there and ask, Why not?
—George Bernard Shaw

What Makes a Good Question?

In action learning, group members continuously strive to ask good questions, even great questions. The better the question, the greater will be the insight gained and solution attained. Often, the best, easiest, and most effective way to ask a good question is simply to build on a previous question or the response to that question. The art and science of careful listening and then generating an open, creative question will quickly and constructively move the group to problem reframing and then strategy development.

What makes a good question? There is no single correct answer to this question, but action learning proponents believe there are a number of essential ingredients to good and powerful questions. Superb questions accomplish a number of wonderful results, as they

▲ Cause us to focus and/or to stretch
▲ Create deep reflection
▲ Challenge taken-for-granted assumptions that prevent us from acting in new and forceful ways
▲ Are difficult to answer and may take courage to ask
▲ Lead to breakthrough thinking
▲ Contain the keys that open the door to great solutions
▲ Are fresh questions raised in "conditions of ignorance, risk, confusion, or when nobody knows what to do next" (Revans, 1982a)
▲ Are supportive, insightful, and challenging
▲ Are unpresumptuous and offered in a sharing spirit
▲ Are selfless, not asked to illustrate the cleverness of the questioner or to generate information or an interesting response for the questioner
▲ Open up the problem owner's view of the situation
▲ Open doors in the mind and get people to think more deeply
▲ Test assumptions and cause people to explore why and how they act
▲ Generate action

Great questions are asked at the time when they will generate the most reflection and learning. "Why" questions are valuable and frequently used in action learning, as they cause us to reflect and to perhaps see things in fresh, unpredictable ways. Questions such as "Why do you think that?" or "Why did this work?" can help the group examine old issues in new, original ways. Other examples of questions that could produce rich responses include the following.

▲ Can that be done in any other way?
▲ What other options can we think of?
▲ What resources have we never used?

▲ What do we expect to happen if we do that?
▲ What would happen if you did nothing at all?
▲ What other options do you have?
▲ What is stopping us?
▲ What happens if . . . ?
▲ Have we ever thought of . . . ?

Action learning groups will know and feel when a great question has been asked. One or more members will spontaneously say, "That's a great question!" Great questions cause us to expressively respond in those or similar words. When a group generates one or more such questions, it can move forward with great confidence that it will reach greater clarity of understanding and imaginative solutions.

A good question is never fully answered. It is not a bolt to be tightened into place, but a seed to be planted and to bear more seed toward the hope of greening the landscape of ideas.
—John Ciardi

Who Asks the Questions?

Everyone! In action learning, questions are not limited to only those with the most expertise or prestige. Questions are asked, and need to be asked, by all members of the group, each of whom has unique perspectives and experiences, each of whom can help the group gain a comprehensive and systemic overview of the problem that allows the group to reframe it and then begin developing the most strategic and innovative solutions.

The problem presenter should and must also ask questions. If she only responds to questions, she will feel like she is on trial. Of course, it is natural that the initial questions be addressed to the problem presenter, as she is the source of vital information needed by the group. However, as soon as possible, the presenter should begin asking questions of the other group members. This is important because it demonstrates to the group that the problem presenter now has sufficient confidence in the group to seek members' ideas, and that she has not predetermined a solution. By asking questions of the group, the problem presenter changes the communication dynamics from a wheel hub (presenter) with spokes (other group members who interact only with the hub) to an interaction in which everyone interacts with everyone else. It is generally at this juncture that the problem moves from the presenter to the entire group. The problem is now in the center of the table for everyone to examine rather than in the mind of the problem presenter. Once group ownership is achieved, greater energy, commitment, and creativity in solving the problem will occur.

Reflection and Reflective Inquiry

The quiet time between questions and responses provides opportunities for group members to examine assumptions and to find common perspectives. For reflective inquiry to occur, there must be space for people to stand back and to unfreeze their presuppositions and basic assumptions. Reflection does not come easily or naturally. In most group settings, attempts to create reflection fail. In action learning groups, however, reflection is continuous and natural. Action learning deliberately carves out the time and creates the conditions for reflecting and listening. The expectation on all members to ask questions and to carefully listen to the responses develops the habit of reflective inquiry within the group as well as in individuals' lives.

Reflection involves recalling, thinking about, pulling apart, making sense, and trying to understand. Reflective inquiry challenges one's programmed knowledge, or what Schein (1997) refers to as "theories in use." This type of inquiry does not deny the importance of programmed knowledge, but it does provide the opportunity for group members to introduce new knowledge. Mezirow (1991) points out that reflection involves bringing one's assumptions, premises, criteria, and schemata into consciousness and vigorously critiquing them.

Reflective inquiry generates mutual support for group members, as they need to listen intently to one another. It is the key to transformative learning. Schön (1983) describes the elements of reflection: (a) diagnosis (ability to frame or make sense of a problem), (b) testing (engaging in experimentation and reflection to test alternative solutions), and (c) the courage to act and to be responsible for one's actions. Reflection plays a role in all stages of the learning cycle described by Kolb (1984), as shown in Figure 1.

Hammer and Stanton (1997) note that organizations and groups can fail in a variety of ways, but these failures all share one underlying cause: a failure to reflect. Authors such as Kotter (1998) and Kouzes and Posner (2002) see reflection as indispensable for leadership development, since it enables leaders to better know themselves.

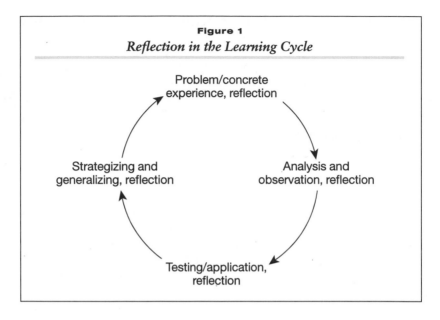

Figure 1
Reflection in the Learning Cycle

Problem/concrete
experience, reflection

Analysis and
observation, reflection

Testing/application,
reflection

Strategizing and
generalizing, reflection

Dialogue and Reflective Inquiry

Dialogue is a special kind of communication in which listening and learning are prized above talking, persuading, and selling. In dialogue, there is a balance between advocacy and inquiry. Advocacy is our natural tendency to push our agenda, whereas inquiry is our attempt through questions to identify the assumptions and perspectives of others. Dialogue encourages win-win situations and does not focus on trying to convince others. Dialogue is very different from debate or discussion, as Table 3 shows.

Dialogue allows the group to tap the collective wisdom of its members and to see the situation more as a whole than as fragmented parts. In dialogue there is an emphasis on asking questions rather than posing solutions, on gaining shared meaning rather than imposing one's own meaning.

In dialogue, every person's ideas are listened to and respected by other members of the group. There is a common pool of information. Dialogue is a special form of conversation that affirms the person-to-person relationship between discussants and acknowledges their collective right and intellectual capacity to make sense of the world. Out of this social sharing of knowledge emerge the seeds of innovation, of some new and imaginative insights that may lead to unexpected but valuable ideas.

Table 3   *Dialogue Versus Debate/Discussion*

Dialogue	Debate/Discussion
Seeing the whole among the parts; seeking the connections between the parts	Breaking issues/problems into parts; seeing distinctions between the parts
Inquiring into assumptions	Justifying/defending assumptions
Learning through inquiry and disclosure	Persuading, selling, telling
Creating shared meaning among many	Gaining agreement on one meaning

Dialogue involves the suspension of opinions and criticism, and instead promotes a creative exploration of issues and problems. Dialogue promotes collective thinking, a positive "teamthink" process. The group now has the potential to co-create meaning as a common understanding is developed. Dialogue brings people to a new way of perceiving an issue that may be of concern to all. That new understanding might include an identification of what actions should be taken or decisions made individually and collectively (Dixon, 1996).

Dialogue involves a relationship. Central to the concept of dialogue is the idea that through the interaction, people acknowledge the wholeness, not just the utility, of others (Dixon, 1996). The focus is on acquiring greater understanding and attaining shared meaning. Dialogue is based on the principle that the human mind is capable of using logic and reason to understand the world, rather than having to rely on the interpretation of someone who claims authority through force, tradition, superior intellect, or divine rights.

Dialogue is an affirmation of the intellectual capability not only of the individual, but also of the collective. It acknowledges that everyone is blind to his or her own tacit assumptions and needs the help of others to see them. It acknowledges that each person, no matter how smart or capable, sees the world from a particular perspective and that there are other legitimate perspectives that could inform that view.

Isaacs (1993) notes that dialogue is more than a set of techniques for improving organizations, enhancing communications, building consensus, or solving problems. It is based on the principle that conception and implementation are intimately linked, with a core of common meaning. During the dialogue process, "people learn to think together—not just in the sense of analyzing a shared problem or creating new pieces of shared knowledge, but in the sense of occupying a collective sensibility, in which the thoughts, emotions, and resulting actions belong not to one individual, but to all of them together"

(p. 25). Through dialogue people can begin to move into coordinated patterns of action and start to act in an aligned way. They can begin to see how to fit parts into a larger whole.

Dialogue and Innovative Thinking in Action Learning

Dialogue is a critical part of the action learning process because it joins people with diverse perspectives; it helps to connect possible solutions to the problem and possible actions with the learning. It is not easy for a group to engage in dialogue, as most people find it difficult to hear an assumption that contradicts their own. Holding on to and defending assumptions gets in the way of dialogue. Action learning's insistence on the use of questions and the reflective inquiry process enables individuals to more easily and effectively engage in dialogue. Dialogue helps remove barriers among participants, as people genuinely seek to engage in open, honest communication.

The practice of dialogue requires a group climate that is open and respectful of individuals and in which information is shared. In an action learning environment, members are free from coercion, and everyone has equal opportunity to challenge the ideas of others. Without such a climate, it is unlikely that the group members would expend the energy or incur the necessary risks to effectively and innovatively solve the problem.

Dialogue is particularly important with the kinds of tough issues often faced by action learning groups. When there is tension or a difficult dilemma to resolve, people are like electrons at high temperatures. They collide and move at cross-purposes. Dialogue, on the other hand, seeks to produce a cooler, shared environment by refocusing the group's attention. Groups tend to go through several stages on their way to achieving dialogue.

1. The *invitation stage* occurs when a group comes together. At this stage, the individuals bring with them a wide range of tacit, unexpressed differences in perspectives (similar to the blind men with the elephant).
2. At the *conversation stage,* the people begin to interact. The word *conversation* is derived from the Latin word *conversare,* "to turn together." In action learning, this is the stage in which the group "turns together" to seek a common understanding of the problem in an effort to reframe it.
3. The *deliberation stage* begins at the point when the group seeks to make choices.

Asking Questions in Other Cultures

Isabel Rimanocy

I have had two very different experiences with cultures not accustomed to accepting questions. In Thailand, questions can be seen as challenging the opinion of another person, and rule number one is that no one should "lose face." My experience led me to reframe the question as a gift for someone, as a sign of interest and curiosity. This reframing totally changed the perception of the question, and the group easily adopted the questioning process. In northern Europe, I was working with pragmatic engineers who initially were upset that they would get questions instead of answers and solutions. I trusted the action learning process and by the end of the second session, I was surprised to hear participants saying that "my life is divided into before and after this program, before and after I started using questions." A deep transformational impact had taken place in those individuals.

---

4. The *suspension stage* requires group members to suspend their views and thereby loosen the grip of their certainty about all views, including their own. At this stage, the group begins to question assumptions.
5. The *dialogue stage* (*dialogue* is a Greek word translated as "the flow of meaning") occurs when the group chooses to live in chaos rather than certainty. During this stage, the group may feel like it is in a giant washing machine. Certainty and conclusions are difficult to manage. However, the group recognizes that there is no need to panic, and if it listens and inquires, clarity will emerge from the chaos, and creativity will occur in the decisions that need to be made by the group.

The Poetry and Art of Asking Great Questions

The ability to ask powerful and challenging questions is an art as well as a science. The science is simply to listen carefully to the preceding question and/or response(s) to that question and build on it (rather than focus on your own interests). The art is to create questions that are truly open and fresh. Like a great poem, the question may be interpreted in a way not intended by the questioner, but may lead to ideas not considered by either party. The seeds to great solutions are thus contained in the words of those great questions. And like great poetry, great questions require time and openness to be truly appreciated. Action learning, through the questioning and reflective processes, taps the best of science and the best of art to generate practical but innovative and imaginative solutions to problems.

Checklist for Questions and Reflection

▲ Are we using open, reflective, and probing questions?

▲ Are they fresh, clarifying, timely, and supportive?

▲ Do we avoid closed, multiple, and leading questions?

▲ Is everyone involved in the questioning?

▲ Do we provide sufficient time between questions?

▲ Did we jump to solutions before framing the problem via questions?

▲ Are we questioning to solve the problem or to impress?

▲ Is there reflective time between questions and comments?

▲ Is listening attentive and open, or is it evaluative and inattentive?

▲ Are we filtering out what the person is saying?

▲ Do we listen without interruption?

▲ Are we viewing each other as learning resources?

▲ Do we give an interpretation of what is said rather than an accurate response?

▲ Do we make and convey assumptions beyond what is said?

▲ What is the level of interest in listening to each other and to oneself?

▲ Are we open to new ways of doing things?

▲ Are new insights arising, and are people making connections with the diversity of questions and opinions being offered?

CHAPTER

5

Action Strategies

An essential part of action learning groups is for them to take action and to learn from that action. Actions involve what occurs within the action learning sessions (problem reframing, establishing goals, developing strategies) and, what is more important, what occurs outside of the action learning meetings (testing, gaining support and resources, taking action). Unless action is taken, the group can never be sure that its strategies and ideas were effective and that the members had, in fact, learned while they were working as a team.

One must learn by doing the thing, for though you think you know it, you have no certainty until you try.
—Aristotle

Learning is significant only if we take some type of action as a result of that learning (thus the action learning axiom of "there is no real learning without action, just as there should be no action without learning"). Accordingly, one or more members of the action learning group must have the power to take action themselves or be assured

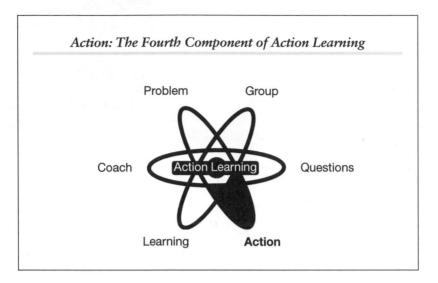

Action: The Fourth Component of Action Learning

that their recommendations will be implemented (barring any significant change in the environment or the group's lack of essential information).

Increasing the quality and scope of knowledge and learning is an inherent part of the action learning process. Organizations should make every effort to afford action learning teams the opportunities to learn from their strategizing, pilot testing, and implementing of plans. Action enhances individual and group learning because it provides a basis and anchor for additional questioning and reflection. As the group assesses and reflects on its actions both within and outside the group, it can determine its level of success and improve the group's knowledge as well as future actions. The learnings gained from the actions should be applied not only to the present problem, but to future tasks and challenges as well.

To know something, but not to use it, is not knowing.
—Buddhist proverb

Approaches to Problem Solving

Groups and individuals may choose between two contrasting approaches to problem solving: *analytic/rationalistic* and *integrative*.

Table 4	*Approaches to Problem Solving*

Analytic/rationalistic	Integrative
One right solution	Multiple right answers
Thinking is separate from action	Thinking requires/exists in action
Goal is to solve problems	Goal is learning from opportunity
Clear problem definition—hypothesis and linear causality	Diffuse problem definition—an issue and multiple causalities
Analysis of factions, reductionist; elimination of possibilities, specific questions; deterministic and sequential	Collecting insights, holistic; integration of possibilities; open questions; associative, intuitive; synchronistic
Objective: find the solution; quality of the answer	Objective: discovery of interrelationships; quality of understanding

Proponents of the *analytic/rationalistic* type of problem solving believe that there is one right solution to a problem. The group should develop a strategy based on a careful analysis of the situation and then determine in a logical fashion the causes of the problem and the solutions to it.

Advocates of the *integrative* approach, on the other hand, believe that there may be multiple right answers. Learning while taking action and acting out the thinking and learning are both equally important. Solving the problem is only part of the goal; learning from the opportunity is also a goal. The group attempts to collect a variety of insights in a holistic manner and to integrate the various possibilities. Intuition, open questions, and free associations are all tools of the integrative process of problem solving. Finding interrelationships between problems and solutions is valuable not only for this problem, but for future problems as well. Table 4 summarizes the differences in these two approaches.

Systems Thinking in Problem Solving

Effective and long-lasting problem solving and strategy setting must be built on the foundation and benefits of systems thinking. Systems thinking, in contrast to linear thinking, is based on a conceptual framework that allows us to see patterns and how to effectively change those patterns. Based in the field of chaos theory, systems thinking focuses on seeing the whole picture (using holistic thinking). It provides a framework for seeing interrelationships rather than linear cause-effect chains, for noticing underlying structures rather than events, for discovering patterns of change rather than snapshots (Senge, 1990).

Systems thinking recognizes that what affects one part of an organization affects other parts in planned and unplanned ways with sometimes surprising and unpredictable consequences. Thus, small, well-focused actions can produce significant, enduring improvements when these actions occur at the right time, in the right place, and with sufficient leverage (Gharajedaghi, 1999). Whereas systems thinking is based on quantum physics, linear thinking is built on Newtonian physics. Linear thinking is much more mechanical, slow, and narrowly focused. Problems are treated as if the environment were predictable and cause and effect could be identified and isolated.

Newtonian Versus Quantum Physics

For nearly three centuries the world and the workplace have been built on Newtonian physics—the physics of cause and effect, of predictability and certainty, of distinct wholes and parts, of reality being what is seen. Newtonian physics is a science of quantifiable determinism, of linear thinking and a controllable future—in sum, a world that does not change too fast or in unexpected ways. In the Newtonian mind-set, people engage in complex planning for a world that they believe is predictable. They continually search for better methods of objectively perceiving the world. This mechanistic and reductionist way of thinking and acting dominates our lives, even though it was disproved by Albert Einstein and others who introduced the scientific community to quantum physics in the 1920s. Margaret Wheatley (1992), author of *Leadership and the New Science,* notes that this old, disproved mind-set in today's world is "unempowering and disabling for all of us."

Quantum physics, on the other hand, deals with the world at the subatomic level, examining the intricate patterns out of which seemingly discrete events arise. Quantum physics recognizes that the universe and every object in it are, in reality, vast empty spaces that are filled with fields and movements that are the basic substance of the universe. Thus relationships between objects and between observers and objects determine reality. The quantum universe is an environment rich in relationships; it is a world of chaos, of process, and not just of objects and things. Quantum physics deals with waves and holograms, of surprises rather than predictions. With an understanding of quantum physics, organizations and teams realize that they cannot predict with certainty, that chaos is part and parcel of reality. The actuality of quantum physics requires us to change the way we think and the way we attempt to solve problems as well as the way we deal with order versus change, autonomy versus control, structure versus flexibility, planning versus flowing. ■

A key to action learning's power is its employment of systems thinking. Action learning acknowledges what scientists proved nearly a hundred years ago, namely, that Newtonian physics does not and cannot explain reality. Action learning recognizes that the old way of thinking and solving problems does not work, especially in today's rapidly changing environment. Action learning therefore utilizes quantum physics, chaos theory, and systems thinking.

Diverse group members who utilize reflective inquiry to work on complex problems are the perfect embodiment of a systems thinking approach to solving problems and developing workable and effective action strategies. The questioning process and diverse perspectives create a natural systems way of responding to complexity. Asking layers of questions and reflecting on responses to those questions forces group members to think beyond symptoms to root causes, to explore a wide array of perspectives. As a result, action learning is holistic and comprehensive in its approach.

Clear and Compact Time Frame

The problem or task assigned to the action learning group is one that should be real and urgent and thus require a clear time frame for the group. Since action learning groups face real time constraints, the opportunity to resolve the issue may exist for only a limited period. Action learning groups should therefore move quickly and judiciously to complete their work.

Depending on external forces as well as internal expectations, the decision or strategy might need to be initiated within a few hours or within a few months. The group therefore might meet only one time for thirty minutes or for three hours. If the target time is a week away and the problem is complex, the group may need to meet eight hours a day for a full week. On the other hand, if the decision point is not imminent (e.g., cut costs by 10 percent by the end of the fiscal year) or the decision and strategy are complex and involve many internal and external players, the group may be able to meet on a part-time basis over several months, perhaps once a week for a few hours. Thus, depending on the circumstances, action learning groups may meet either full time or part time, for a single session or for multiple sessions over several months.

Full-Time Versus Part-Time Programs

Meeting full time allows action learning groups to quickly respond to the problem or crisis assigned to them. They are less likely to be interrupted by other job responsibilities. Top management should seek ways to delay or delegate members' other commitments so that members can concentrate their energies and efforts on solving the problem and developing strategies. Two disadvantages of full-time action learning groups are that (a) there may be insufficient time between or during sessions to collect and confirm needed information, to create and/or maintain necessary support from within the organization, or to test the strategies; and (b) there may not be sufficient time or opportunity for individual members to apply their learnings or to see the personal growth in their leadership and professional competencies.

Part-time action learning groups, on the other hand, have somewhat contrasting benefits and disadvantages. The significant benefit of meeting on a part-time basis is that actions can be taken between sessions and progress can be reported. Difficulties and setbacks can be learned, and new strategies for tackling the problem can be developed. Also, reflections on learnings can occur over a longer period of time. Members will be better able to see the progress/changes in learnings and confidence occurring within themselves, the team, and/or the organization. The disadvantages of part-time groups include (a) membership or enthusiasm is lost over time, (b) the problem is not adequately reframed and resolved within the available time frame, and (c) the context has changed and the organization or individual no longer sees the issue as urgent.

Action Learning at General Electric

To optimize the success of problem solving at General Electric, the following criteria are established for any action learning project.

1. Each action learning project needs to have consistent, high-level champions; otherwise, we will not work on it.
2. Each action learning group should have a real business problem or opportunity that is well-defined and scoped.
3. Quality planning time is critical to final outcome and success of each action learning group.
4. There must be a strong commitment for action learning from GE leaders and action learning members.
5. Follow-up is critical throughout the action learning project.
6. It is important to keep employees involved in implementation, and there must be an established process with checkpoints.

7. Leaders must ensure that employees have the support needed to implement the action plans.
8. We must ensure that there is no overlap or duplication with other ongoing work in the organization.
9. Sponsors should respond positively to the recommendations made by the action learning group unless they are illegal, unethical, or out of bounds, in which case the sponsors should modify the recommendations.
10. Before tasking the action learning group, there should be clear boundaries on what is open to change and what is not (financial, head count, technology enhancements, customers, etc.).
11. Top management should have a clear understanding and orientation on how action learning works. ■

Stages in Action Learning Problem Solving

In action learning, the group goes through four stages from the point of examining the problem to the final implementing of the strategies. The first two stages make up the diagnostic phase, during which the group is exploring questions about what needs to be accomplished, what is preventing the organization from achieving its objective, and how to overcome obstacles. The final two stages represent the strategy and implementation phases. The learning that occurs after each of the four stages, and how the tested and implemented actions can be applied to other parts of the organization, are discussed in Chapter 6.

Stage 1: Understanding and reframing the problem

Stage 2: Framing and formulating the goal

Stage 3: Developing and testing strategies

Stage 4: Taking action and reflecting on the action

Stage 1: Understanding and Reframing the Problem

Understanding the problem is the most important step in problem solving (what good is it to come up with great solutions to the wrong problem?), yet most individuals and groups rush into the search for the answers. This is a natural and normal impulse, as most people are uncomfortable with and do like to spend too much time in ambiguity. As a result, most groups neglect the problem clarification stage and end up either disagreeing over solutions because they have internally diagnosed the problem differently or correctly solving a wrong or less important issue. Both can lead to disastrous results for the individual, team, and/or organization. Thus, it is important that we take time to get agreement on the problem; otherwise, we can never get true agreement on the solutions.

Action learning, through its clear insistence on questioning and gaining consensus on what the problem is, forces the group to spend time on understanding the problem and its context and conditions. The coach does not allow the group to proceed to the problem solution and strategy development stages until the members have questioned the problem thoroughly and reached an agreement about its nature.

In action learning, we recognize that the presenting problem may be neither the real problem nor the most important problem. Members must be open to this possibility. Block (1999) notes that the original problem is rarely the one that is most crucial, and therefore groups who merely accept the initial problem often end up solving a surface problem—one that is unimportant and, if solved, does not resolve the situation. The systems thinking and diverse perspectives approach used in action learning allows groups to thoroughly uncover the layers that surround or camouflage the true problem.

Action learning also recognizes that problems can be understood as a group only through the questioning process. The initially presented problem inevitably contains assumptions, expectations, biases, symptoms, and limited perspectives on the part of both the presenter and the group members. Through questions and reflection, the individuals gradually join together in agreeing on the critical problem and related goal on which the group should spend its energies. Questioning rather than debating results in clear understandings and agreements, in individuals seeing the problem in a similar way.

Experienced problem solvers recognize that in the process of clarifying the presenting problem and moving to the critical problem, we must diverge before we converge—we must see the whole forest (the big picture) before examining the individual trees. To properly explore the problem, we should examine possible causes and consequences to find the basic roots as well as the observable symptoms.

The ground rule "questions before statements" is critical at this stage of problem solving. Asking questions rather than immediately offering solutions unfreezes the group and defuses defensiveness on the part of the problem presenter. Understanding the problem is not solely the burden of the presenter, but is everybody's primary task. Questions help reveal the problem and give the group a systems perspective. When the problem is still unclear and nobody is ready with solutions, asking questions sparks new ideas and possible strategies. The seeds of potential solutions are unconsciously being sown. Thus, we are birthing solutions while we are inquiring of the problem. As the problem becomes more clearly defined, new insights and solutions naturally emerge.

As a result of the entire group questioning the problem as originally presented, the group gradually begins to reframe the problem. Reframing, according to Dilt (1999), helps people to reinterpret problems and find solutions by changing the frame in which the problems are being perceived. Reframing transforms the meaning of the problem by putting it into a new context. By observing a problem from different angles, we can thus reinterpret it. This is important in helping us solve the real problem, so that once it is solved, it can stay solved.

There are two types of approaches to reframing. The first—the *content* approach—changes the meaning of the way a person experiences a situation. Reframing the *context,* on the other hand, helps us to perceive and evaluate the same situation in a different way as we change the meaning of external stimuli.

The action learning coach is often quite active during the problem reframing stage. At the beginning of the session, or at the beginning of each person's problem presentation in multiple-problem sets, she will ask the problem presenter to take only a few moments to describe the problem as he sees and feels it. Later on, before allowing the group to move to setting goals and developing strategies, the coach will check to see if everyone agrees on the crucial problem. She does this by asking each person to write down what he or she believes the problem to be. Members are then asked to state the problem as they understand it, with the problem presenter being the last person to speak. If the group believes there is agreement, they can then move on to the next stage; if not, they continue working on identifying and reframing the problem until consensus has been reached.

It is better to first put your finger on the problem before sticking your nose in it.
—Anonymous

Stage 2: Framing and Formulating the Goal

After the group has reached consensus on the problem, it must determine what the group, the organization, or the individual should strive to achieve. The organization and/or problem presenter authorizes and empowers the action learning group to redefine the problem after a systematic examination of it. Consequently, the group has the responsibility to solve the real and most critical problem rather than merely and meekly accept the given problem. Thus, if the problem is different from what it was originally thought to be, then the target goal or objectives to solve that problem will be different from what was originally expected.

The group should be courageous in selecting a goal it believes is most strategic, has the most staying power, and will solve the real problem with easy-to-leverage results. If the group simply accepts the given problem or task (sometimes we mistakenly do so even when top leadership is expecting us to utilize the time, wisdom, and perspectives of the group), it ends up providing a disservice to the organization by not offering the needed long-term solution, and to the members themselves by missing an opportunity to examine the issue in its depth and complexity and learning from it.

Without power to discard beliefs shown to be wrong, one cannot introduce actions known to be right.
—Reg Revans

With its power and understanding, the group should be ready to move from the reframed problem to the purpose of the group. Remaining focused on the problem will not get the organization where it needs to go. Focusing on the problem rather than the desirable future generates negative, overwhelming, and dissipating energy. Focusing the desired future, however, creates positive energy (Cooperrider, Sorensen, and Yaeger, 2001).

Framing the goal causes the group to shift in three ways: from a problem frame to an outcome frame, from an "it is impossible" frame to an as-if frame, and from a failure frame to a feedback frame. When we move to the goal statement, we move from what is wrong to what we want, from what caused it to what resources we have, from what is too expensive to what is affordable, from "what a waste of time" to "how can we use available resources wisely," from a feeling that our ideas will never work to looking at how we can implement our ideas, and from an unrealistic plan to how we can make the plan more tangible and concrete.

The best and final goal may not be clearly and fully defined at this stage. It may become more refined as the action learning group works on strategies. As in the setting of any goals, the goal should be "SMART," that is, specific, measurable, achievable, realistic, and time bounded. We should also seek goals that are exciting and meaningful to the group and to the organization. As the group develops and aligns the clear goal, the cohesiveness of the group will grow stronger.

Stage 3: Developing and Testing Strategies

During this stage, the action learning group develops both strategic (what things to do) and tactical (how to do it) strategies. Gaining consensus on strategies is much easier if the group has reached agreement on the problem and the goal during stages 1 and 2.

In stage 2, we identified the goal, that is, what we wanted or needed to do. During stage 3 the group becomes more specific and begins exploring questions such as, What will probably work best and why? What resources will we need? What will be the impact of this action? Revans (1983) describes this stage of action learning as the point at which no one knows the right answer, but all are obliged to find it.

In forming an action plan, there are two distinct areas of concern: Is the action appropriate to the problem? and, Is the action doable in the time available? Strategies will simply not get implemented if they are not appropriate or doable. They also will not get implemented if we do not identify the people "who know what we need to know, who can get it implemented, and who care about getting it done." In other words, Who are the people who have the intelligence and insights to ensure that the best steps are being taken, who have the power to ensure that agreed-upon strategies are in fact implemented, and who have the passion and commitment to follow up on the strategies that have been developed? These are the people who know, who care, and who can. These are the folks who are critical in implementing and supporting the strategies developed by the group. If the group's plan is not appropriate and doable, the plan will forever remain a plan.

In examining the strategies, the group needs to identify the obstacles preventing the individual, team, or organization from achieving its goal(s). The group considers which obstacles are most critical, and which, if overcome, will provide the greatest benefit and leverage. Which ones are changeable and which ones can be left alone? It is important that they be examined in a systems-oriented manner.

Many groups use brainstorming to identify a variety of options for resources and application. This approach, however, is built on the Newtonian way of strategizing. It usually results in a long list of possibilities, most of which are totally impractical or absurd, result in busy work, and require a considerable amount of time just to painstakingly examine and discard. On the other hand, the action learning approach of developing strategies by building on each others' questions is based on chaos theory and systems thinking. This approach is more robust, is less time consuming, and systematically enables the group to understand the complexity and derive the best solutions from within the chaos.

Another dynamic that occurs frequently as groups seek to solve problems is the tendency of various individuals to provide anecdotes and examples of their experiences and successes or failures. In action learning, we seek to move people from anecdotal to analytical communications for two reasons: the anecdotal approach slows down the

Action Learning Successes at
William Halley Elementary School, Lorton, Virginia

Jan Funk, Principal

Action learning has served as a wonderful vehicle to assist the staff at William Halley Elementary School in solving a number of important problems. One major concern related to improving SOL test scores, which is necessary to ensure state accreditation. Over a four-month period, the staff met in vertical teams (teams that included teachers and staff) to determine what was going well and where change needed to occur in order to raise test scores. From this continuous dialogue, eight learning teams were created to research a variety of programs, models, and strategies. At the end of the year, each team shared the outcomes of its research with the entire staff, and we selected the following two challenges as being most critical and strategic.

▲ Fragmentation. In grades five and six, fragmentation, or "time to teach," was a major issue. With all of the pull-out programs—band, strings, chorus, gifted/talented, peer mediation, patrols, and SCA—there were few blocks of teaching time during which the entire class was present. Classroom management took a significant amount of time from instruction. Two action learning teams were created to determine how to resolve these concerns. Volunteers met during the summer to puzzle over the creation of a schedule to reduce fragmentation. After several days and sessions, a block schedule emerged that now gives the teachers more than four hours of uninterrupted teaching time.

▲ Positive classroom behavior. Another action learning team tackled the concern of maintaining positive classroom behavior. With the help of a grant from Johns Hopkins University, the action learning team developed a schoolwide Positive Discipline Program. This program provides teachers with strategies and techniques that are unified throughout the school. A Behavior Support Team works with teachers who need additional assistance with difficult students. Students and parents were made aware of the program through a handbook designed by the team. As a result of this action learning project, discipline referrals have been tremendously reduced.

At Halley Elementary, not only did action learning successfully address two major concerns, but also teacher leaders began to emerge, and everyone felt part of a culture of learners. Teacher fulfillment as well as SOL scores improved, and Halley enjoys full state accreditation.

group and it puts attention on the person with the story rather than on the problem.

Often more than one strategy will need to be developed and then tested. Multiple alternatives will increase the possibilities of better actions and results. As the various alternatives are considered, the action learning group should carefully examine issues such as how realistic and cost-effective each alternative may be, what new problems are created by the alternative, and which ones have more passion, power, and knowledge.

Most problem-solving groups tend to use only programmed knowledge (the knowledge they brought with them to the group) as they begin considering and developing action strategies. Programmed knowledge is often embedded in the past and is therefore not likely to match precisely the unique needs of the new problem or situation. The action learning process, however, incorporates the programmed knowledge of each member with the newly generated knowledge created within the group. Thus action learning groups are more successful in developing innovative, high-impact strategies that respond specifically and strategically to the problem being addressed.

Plans and strategies, whenever possible, should be tested to determine their impact and effectiveness. Strategies should be selected that provide optimum leverage at the least cost to the individual, group, or organization. If systems thinking is applied, small, well-focused actions result in significant, enduring improvements (e.g., adjusting the direction of a space shuttle by a few millimeters before liftoff causes more directional change than an adjustment thousands of miles in space). High-leverage changes, however, are often not obvious to individuals within the environment in which they are operating. Thus we tend to choose strategies that are closer in time and space. Testing strategies by the action learning group also allows for final opportunities to adapt or develop new plans.

Pilot actions will enable the group to gain greater assurance of ultimate success in the actions taken as well as provide higher levels of learning. Of course, there will be occasional risks in action learning, but they are prudent risks because they are taken with much more information about the possible consequences of the action.

Action learning holds that the most significant learning occurs when members reflect on the results of their actions and not just on their planning. In action learning, we recognize that actions are also learning opportunities. Only by testing their ideas in practice will members know whether the proposed strategies are effective and practical, whether any issues have been overlooked, what questions should have been asked, and what they can learn and apply to this and other projects and activities.

Stage 4: Taking Action and Reflecting on the Action

Taking action is an important element of any action learning group's work. If the group is merely making recommendations, the result will be diminished commitment as well as diminished learning. Revans (1983) notes that just as one cannot learn how to serve a tennis ball unless he hits it, an individual or group cannot learn unless there is the opportunity to implement.

Action learning is built on a framework designed to capture and build on what exists in the real world rather than in the pure, detached, analytical, and rational world of what should be. Smith (2001) writes that in action learning, we "promote cogitation and insightful inquiry with perceptive partners in situations where solutions are not always obvious, and by leaving responsibility for implementation of the solution in the participant's hands, it is particularly suited to enhancing leadership capabilities" (p. 36).

At the end of each session, the group agrees to take concrete, specific actions. The steps developed include the specifics of who, what, where, and when, as well as the measurable, the visible, and the worthwhile. These actions should be recorded and then referred to at the beginning of the subsequent session of the action learning group.

To ensure that the individual or group will develop actions before the end of the session, the coach asks what actions will be taken. If the coach senses that the group may be running out of time, she will remind the group of the necessity of generating action before concluding the session. If a session ends with no actions decided on, the group will not be able to fully utilize the time between sessions. There will also be lost opportunities for learnings that could occur as a result of reflecting on the success or failures or unexpected consequences of the actions. Finally, if the individual (in multiple-problem sets) or the group members do not take action between sessions, the group may feel that the problem is not urgent and that they are wasting their time. At the next session, the group will probably be less enthusiastic when working on the problem and less creative in developing action strategies.

Cutting the Costs of Moving at a Malaysian Business College

A budget of $100,000 had been established to move all the equipment and other furnishings from the current site to new buildings across the city of Kuala Lumpur. An action learning group composed of teachers, students, and administrative personnel explored a variety of options and eventually decided that much of the moving could be done by themselves. A careful, item-by-item plan was developed. Over a weekend, the entire move was completed for less than $20,000, in a shorter period of time, and with new cross-functional teams and greater collegiality among all the people of the college. ■

Distribution of Time in the Four Stages of Action Learning

Every action learning group and every problem has its own unique dynamics and flow, complexity, and challenge. Thus, the amount of time and energy devoted to each of the stages will vary. Normally, especially when the group is first formed, stages 1 and 2—reframing the problem and framing the goal—will consume much of the first meeting. The group naturally needs to gather information and seek clarification of the problem before it can begin searching for the most powerful purpose. At subsequent meetings the group may need to spend only a few minutes to reconfirm the problem and goal, mainly to check that no new forces or circumstances have altered the situation, thereby creating new and different problems, which may then necessitate changes in the goal. Generally, the bulk of time at subsequent meetings will be spent working on stage 3, namely, the development of strategies.

Many problem-solving groups follow these same four stages. Action learning groups, however, devote more effort and time than do other groups to stage 1. In action learning, we recognize that if we can first agree on the problem, then it is much easier to agree on solutions. For example, if a group has a total of sixty minutes to work on the first three stages, up to forty-five minutes may be devoted to gaining consensus as to what the real problem is.

Typically, groups are rushed into developing strategies (stage 3) and may spend forty-five minutes advocating a strategy based on members' understanding of the problem. But if everyone understands the problem in a slightly different way, it is difficult, if not possible, to get agreement on the goal, much less on the strategies to achieve that goal. Whereas, if there is agreement on the real problem, then agreement on strategies becomes easier and less painful.

Action Framework

Smith (2001) has developed a framework to assist action learning teams to carefully plan action strategies. He proposes that performance systems in action learning be based on three elements—*focus, will,* and *capability.* The resulting performance level achieved by the systems depends on the interactions and interdependencies of these elements. *Focus* represents a clear understanding of the problem and the performance proposed. Focus deals with the question "What are we trying to accomplish?" as well as information-gathering questions that ask what, how, who, where, when, and why. *Will* represents the strength of intent to take action on the performance determined in focus. It is associated with attitudes, emotions, beliefs, and mind-sets, the "Who cares?" question. *Capability* represents the wherewithal to transform into reality the performance defined in the focus. *Capability* is associated with resources such as skills, infrastructure, budgets, tools, and physical assets. In exemplifying this action learning model, Smith provides the following two examples.

▲ At an organizational level, *focus* might represent the firm's strategic plans to enter a market; *will* would reflect the organization's cultural potential to support the new initiative, and *capability* would relate to the firm's asset position on entering that market.

▲ In marketing, *focus* might represent dividing up a sales territory; *will* would be associated with how the participants and members of the sales organization at large would feel about the proposed new segmentation; and *capability* would address the skill requirement and infrastructure required for the newly segmented sales force to function adequately.

Developing Training at Fairfax County Public Schools (FCPS)

Eight staff members of FCPS, including principals, teachers, and HR staff, had two hours in an action learning session to develop a long-term training program for principals and assistant principals. Despite the impatience of some members, the group kept focusing on determining the real problem and the real goals. It took more than sixty minutes to reach an agreement about the true problem and the most important goals. But in the final thirty minutes, the group identified strategies and developed the outlines of a project that ultimately led to a five-million-dollar grant from the Reader's Digest Foundation for leadership development in FCPS. ■

Systems and Tools for Solving Problems and Developing Strategies

The context for problem solving in action learning, according to Revans (1971, 1982a), involves what he refers to as *Systems Alpha, Beta,* and *Gamma.*

▲ *System Alpha* is analogous to situation analysis. Group members need to understand the system within which the problem resides. They must be involved in examining the nature of the value systems, both the external system that affects the decisions being made and the internal system in which the manager works.

▲ *System Beta* refers to the negotiation and implementation of a solution and involves (a) survey, (b) hypothesis, (c) experiment, (d) audit, and (e) review. This system is equated to learning systems of recognition, prima facie acceptance, rehearsal, verification, and conviction.

▲ *System Gamma* refers to the mental predisposition that the individual, group, or organization brings to the situation. Individuals and groups must continually check their expectations of what should be happening against what is actually happening. Insofar as they are able to identify the discrepancies between what they first took to be the condition and what experience suggests the condition actually was, and insofar as they are able to change this perception accordingly, we may say that they are learning.

Although action learning does not encourage a profusion of problem-solving tools, there certainly are occasions when they should be utilized. Such tools could include rational analysis, audit methods, double-Q diagrams, Pareto charts, force field analysis, and mind mapping.

The Power of Action in Action Learning

The proof of the pudding for users of action learning is the quality of the solutions generated by action learning groups. As demonstrated by the cases and endorsements throughout this book, action learning has indeed produced innovative strategies that have saved companies millions of dollars, expanded global markets, developed new products and processes, and solved complex management issues. From Chicago to Cairo and from Bangkok to Boston, action learning has provided amazing results for organizations such as Unilever, British Airways, Boeing, Caterpillar, Novartis, DuPont, Nokia, the Canadian Royal Mounted Police, and the U.S. Army. The power of action learning will continue to generate successes as more companies are introduced to the dynamics and elements of the four stages of action learning.

Checklist for Problem Reframing, Goal Formulation, Strategy Development, and Action Taking

Problem reframing
▲ What is the quality of the problem solving?
▲ Has the problem been reframed?
▲ Is it a technical or adaptive problem?
▲ Did we ask fresh questions?
▲ Is the presenting problem the real problem or only a symptom of the problem?
▲ What is the level of commitment to solving the problem?

Goal formulation
▲ Will achieving this goal or objective solve the real problem?
▲ Will this goal keep the problem solved?
▲ What is the leverage gained and impact achieved by this goal?
▲ Will the goal stretch the individual, team, and/or organization?
▲ Does the goal complement and support other goals of the organization?

Strategy development
▲ Have the obstacles been identified?
▲ Are we committed to innovative, high-quality solutions and strategies rather than quick solutions?
▲ Have we tapped the sources of power, passion, and knowledge?
▲ Have outside resources and links that may be needed been identified?
▲ Have the impact and consequences of the strategies been carefully considered?
▲ Is this the best-leveraged solution?

Action taking
▲ Are actions to be taken a part of each meeting?
▲ Are the actions clear as to who, what, and when?
▲ Are they recorded and then reviewed at the next meeting?
▲ Have we gained any learnings from actions taken?
▲ Are strategies being implemented?

CHAPTER

6

Individual, Team, and Organizational Learning

Organizations and leaders around the world now recognize that knowledge is their most valuable asset in this competitive and unpredictable global environment. Programs and means that can create and capture relevant and immediately applicable learnings will appeal to any company that is concerned about both its short-term survival and long-term success.

The power and attractiveness of action learning lie in action learning's ability to increase and expand the knowledge of an organization at the same time that it is solving critical, urgent, and complex problems. Solving problems provides immediate short-term benefits to an organization, team, or individual (and is important in getting organizational buy-in for setting up company-based action learning programs), but the greater, long-term value of action learning to the company is the application of new learnings on a systemwide basis—throughout the organization and in the professional lives of the participants.

Dilworth (1998) notes that the learning that occurs in action learning has greater strategic value for the organization than the immediate tactical advantage of solving a problem. In action learning, we recognize that learning is ultimately much more valuable than solving the

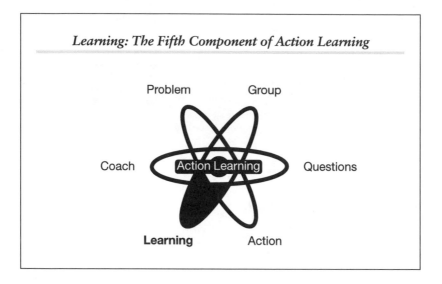

Learning: The Fifth Component of Action Learning

Problem   Group

Coach   Action Learning   Questions

Learning   Action

problem itself; for example, solving a particular reengineering problem may be worth $1 million; applying that knowledge throughout the organization may be worth $10 million. Then applying the new leadership and team skills developed in the action learning program by the group members may be worth $100 million as each person applies the new skills over the course of his or her career with the organization. The collective application of the developed competencies in one organization has a multiplying and leveraging impact that can transform the company and enable it to make quantum leaps with its powerful competitive advantage. Thus, learning as an organization leverages knowledge throughout the enterprise.

Action learning provides a special, valuable kind of knowledge and learning. The degree and quality of learning are not unexpected, because they develop via real people working with each other on real problems, searching for knowledge that will effect positive change. Learning is emphasized continuously in the action learning process, since it is the increased learning of the team that ultimately makes it more effective in problem solving and decision making.

Responsibility of Each Member to Learn

Because of the value of learning, members in action learning groups are advised at the very first session that their learning will be as important

---

Speeding Work and Learning at Siemens

Peter Pribilla, Head of Corporate Human Resources

The speed at which a corporation can learn and employ new knowledge is a decisive factor in corporate success. It is not enough to learn and to work. Learning and work must be integrated. Action learning addresses this challenge very efficiently.

---

to the group and to the organization as solving the problem. If they become smarter as individuals and as a team, they will become capable of achieving breakthrough thinking and groundbreaking solutions. Thus, as a condition of membership in the action learning program, individuals accept responsibility for their own, the group's, and the organization's learning. The group is informed that time will be set aside specifically for learning, and a person (the coach) will carve out and manage this time.

Dilworth (1998) emphasizes the importance of learning for building long-term capabilities. He adds, "Fresh thinking and new learning are needed if we are to avoid responding to today's problems with yesterday's solutions while tomorrow's challenges engulf us" (p. 35).

We had the experience, but missed the meaning.
—T. S. Eliot

Creating, Developing, and Capturing Learning

A number of conditions and circumstances are created in the action learning process that generate high levels of learning. Of greatest impact is the carefully planned, created, and sustained environment that is generated by the six elements of action learning, especially through the actions of the coach. The action learning coach is granted the authority and power to intervene whenever she senses an opportunity for the group to learn. Through a series of reflective questions (as we note in greater detail in Chapter 7), she guides the group in its learning process. The coach enables group members to become more conscious of and competent in several areas: gaining new knowledge and information; reasoning differently; behaving more effectively in groups; gaining greater understanding of their motives; altering beliefs, values, and basic assumptions; and acknowledging feelings and their impact.

The coach helps to provide a safe environment or "practice field" in which reflecting and learning can occur. Within the group, it is safe to be vulnerable, to learn, and to take risks. Failures within the group or in solving a problem are seen as wonderful opportunities to learn rather than events that must be hidden or ignored.

Members are encouraged to recognize the potential of all situations to provide learning opportunities. Individuals are provided the time to reflect on their effectiveness and helpfulness to the group. Problems and crises become valuable occasions for learning and development (McGill and Beaty, 1995).

Since individuals in the group know they are there to learn as well as to solve the problem, there is an expectant mood and a disposition to learn. Learning is rewarded through recognition and improved skills. Members are expected to contribute to each other's learning. The urgent and important problem serves as an energizing impetus to build our learning capabilities.

The questioning process creates the physiological and psychological conditions for learning and thus augments learning opportunities. In addition, the requirement for the group to take action forces members to test their ideas and theories in reality. Since everyone is expected and encouraged to learn, the group environment is conducive to change and growth. As Sandelands (1998) observes, learning is synergistically effective with a group of colleagues who are responsible together.

Action learning encourages self-critical reflection and feedback from frank and honest fellow set members (Zuber-Skerritt, 1995). Group learning is generated as members discuss, share, and pool their ambitions and experiences, thus creating a gestalt in which the benefits of group synergy can be reaped (Smith, 2001).

How Action Learning Generates Learning

Learning is continuous and pervasive in action learning—it takes place throughout the whole action learning process. Opportunities to question, reflect, and learn occur during each of the stages described by Kolb (1984), both as the group works on the problem (Figure 2) and while the group reflects on its interactions and activities (Figure 3). In

Cycles of Learning

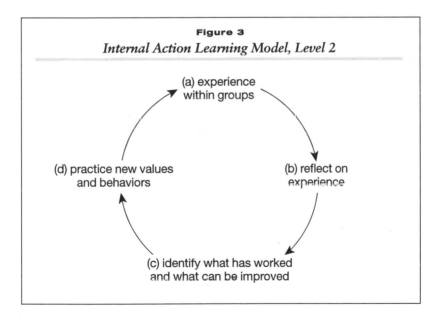

Figure 2
Kolb Learning Model, Level 1

(a) concrete experience

(b) observe and reflect

(c) generalize and conceptualize

(d) test and experiment

Figure 3
Internal Action Learning Model, Level 2

(a) experience within groups

(b) reflect on experience

(c) identify what has worked and what can be improved

(d) practice new values and behaviors

action learning, we create knowledge through concrete experience, observing and reflecting on this experience, forming generalizations from experiences, and testing the implications of those generalizations in new experiences. Let's examine the learning at each of the four stages and at each of the two levels.

Concrete Experience

Level 1: The concrete experience of the group is the problem or task that the group must resolve. One or all of the members may have actually been working on the problem before joining the group. The problem has become urgent and important to them as the organization (or individual in a multiple-problem set) is depending on the group to develop a strategy to overcome the problem.

Level 2: All of the members create a new, real group experience as they jointly reframe the problem, frame the goals, develop strategies, and take action. The group, in a sense, returns to this stage after it has taken actions and thereby generated additional shared concrete experiences.

Observe and Reflect

Level 1: Through the reflective inquiry process, group members examine their problem solving and action strategies to begin assessing their degree of success.

Level 2: The learning coach asks the group to reflect on the quality of their decision making, group interaction skills, and individual learnings. New individual and team competencies are developed based on self-reflection and the perspectives offered by members of the group.

Generalize and Conceptualize

Level 1: At this stage the group determines if and how it can apply the proposed strategies and actions to other similar and dissimilar situations in the organization or in members' personal lives.

Level 2: The group identifies norms and principles and strategies that will make it a better group as it works on this or future problems. In addition, individuals examine how these concepts may apply to other situations in their lives, to see if there might be what Mezirow (1991) describes as "transformative learning experiences."

Test and Experiment

Level 1: The group pilot tests its strategies to see how effectively they will resolve the problem. The group also may test the implications of its newly developed concepts in other contexts as well as discuss whether the new theories might work in future situations.

Level 2: The group reflects, with the help of the action learning coach, on whether its new and modified behaviors and values will enhance the groups' capabilities if it works on additional problems.

Types of Knowledge Created by Action Learning

In its efforts to generate as much knowledge as is needed to solve the current and future problems, the action learning group seeks to create and/or capture the following types of knowledge.

▲ *Know what:* identifying what knowledge is needed
▲ *Know how:* learning how the knowledge must be processed
▲ *Know why:* determining why specific information is needed
▲ *Know where:* knowing where to find needed information
▲ *Know when:* identifying the times when certain information is needed

These types of knowledge are gathered, selected, and then applied in a systemic and system-oriented manner at appropriate stages of the action learning process.

Tacit Versus Explicit Knowledge

Many organizations fail to tap the rich knowledge base or intellectual capital present in the brains of their own employees—what Nonaka (1994) calls "tacit knowledge" in contrast to "explicit knowledge," which already exists outside the internal knowledge of an individual. Sources of tacit knowledge include an individual's expertise, memories, beliefs, and insights. This kind of knowledge is usually difficult to communicate or explain and, as a result, is used only by the individual; thus, its potential benefits to the organization are minimal. Action learning, however, through the reflective inquiry process, the focus on both action and learning, and the questioning approach of the coach converts this tacit knowledge to explicit knowledge so that it becomes available for the team and ultimately for the organization to utilize, resulting in tremendous new assets and capabilities for both.

Programmed Knowledge and Group-Created Knowledge

In addition to converting tacit knowledge into explicit knowledge, the action learning process interweaves the knowledge that each individual brings into the group (tacit or explicit) with the new knowledge created by the group as it reframes the problem, develops strategies, and takes action. The knowledge brought into the group (also referred to as *programmed knowledge,* or *P,* in action learning) is combined with questions *(Q),* which generates new knowledge. The continuous reflection *(R)* results in further and deeper learning and wisdom.

Action learning elicits relevant information from group members and the context, rather than merely disseminating what a trainer or teacher thinks is important. Knowledge is likewise tapped at the points where it is needed. Experience itself, as we know, is a very slippery teacher. Most of the time we have experiences from which we never learn. Experience combined with group reflection, however, enables the group to throw a net around experiences and capture slippery but critical knowledge and learning (Smith, 2001).

Competencies Developed in Action Learning

The remarkable power of action learning is demonstrated by its ability to simultaneously develop learning and skills at the individual level (both for each individual's professional development and for the leader), at the group level, and at the organizational level. Action learning thus can help individuals to improve their lives; groups to better implement their functions; and organizations to leverage that knowledge, with increased staff, leader, and group competencies, to better achieve companywide success.

Individual and Professional Development

The growth of each individual is important to the ultimate understanding and solving of the problem that has been given to the group. As Revans (1980) notes, if the group members are unable to change themselves, they will not be able to change what goes on around them. He writes: "One cannot change the system . . . unless one is also changed in the process, since the logical structure of both changes is in correspondence with each other. The change in the system we call action; that in the self we call learning, so that learning to act effectively is also learning how to learn effectively" (p. 277).

The action taken on a problem changes both the problem and the people acting on it. Marsick and O'Neil (1999) point out that it is the action that generates the learning. While the group is working on the challenge via the action learning process, it develops its internal capacity to learn as well as to learn how to learn. The more we understand ourselves, our mind-sets, our strengths, and our areas needing improvement, the better we are able to reason and solve problems. Morris (1991, p. 74) notes that "action learning provides moments of truth that stick in the memory, and may provide a turning point in one's life and the life of the organization."

In action learning, individuals gain not only an immense amount of knowledge, but also those skills and competencies that are most relevant to and needed by the organization. Such skills include critical reflection, inquiry and questioning, systems thinking, active listening, self-awareness, empathy, problem solving, decision making, presenting, and facilitating. Other valuable competencies developed by action learning are the ability to focus simultaneously on the problem/action and learning, the ability to give and receive feedback, self-discipline, and self-management.

Self-knowledge is critical for any aspect of professional development. As we all know, learning about ourselves can feel threatening, and we resist it if it tends to change our self-image, especially in a less than positive way. In action learning this threat is reduced to a level at which the fear no longer acts as such a strong barrier to gaining self-insight. This occurs because action learning provides safe "practice areas," along with the guidance and reflective questioning of the coach, that emphasize both personal responsibility for learning and also a supportive and challenging environment with fellow group members.

Action learning is concerned with empowering people to become critically conscious of their values, assumptions, actions, interdependencies, rights, and prerogatives so that they can act in a substantially rational way as active partners in producing their reality. Action learning creates an emancipatory kind of learning as it obliges group members to become aware of their own value systems, thereby leading people, as Revans (1983) notes, to "undeceive themselves."

An important part of self-learning is becoming aware of, and changing as necessary, one's beliefs, values, and basic assumptions. A tenet of action learning is that the individual knows more than anyone else what he has learned. And if given time and support, he will discover and develop that learning. In addition, the individual receives comprehensive feedback from other group members and from the results of the problem-solving actions.

Sveiby (1997) defines knowledge as "the capacity to act" (p. 37). True knowledge according to Davenport and Prusak (1998) is action oriented. Individuals who have experienced action learning are encouraged, enabled, and expected to put their newly acquired knowledge and skills into action in their daily lives and throughout their organizations.

Learning and skills acquired by individuals in an action learning group are easily and frequently applied to day-to-day activities. For example, after interacting with a customer on the telephone, the alumnus of action learning will begin to reflect: "How did that conversation go?" "What went well?" "How could I do better next time with this customer as well as with other customers?" Or, as he is interacting with a fellow employee, the seasoned action learning person may ask his colleague, "Is this meeting achieving what we want it to?" "What have we done well thus far?" "How can we improve it?" The changes and improvements in individual behavior of those who have participated in an action learning program can be quite remarkable.

Developing Global Leadership Competencies at Boeing

The Global Leadership Program using action learning debuted in 1999 as one of several tools to enhance Boeing's ability to operate as a global company and to develop leadership competencies within the executive population. The action learning program is targeted to develop executive skills within three categories of global competencies: (1) most-critical competencies (adapting, thinking globally, building relationships, inspiring trust, leading courageously, aligning the organization, influencing, and negotiating), (2) very important competencies (shaping strategy, fostering open and effective communication, attracting and developing talent, driving for stakeholder success, demonstrating vision, using sound judgment), and (3) important competencies (driving execution, inspiring and empowering, working cross-functionally, focusing on quality and continuous improvement, applying financial acumen). ■

Leadership Learning

One of the expectations of most organization-based action learning programs is that the process will develop the leadership competencies of the group members. Most organizational theorists and practitioners agree that new leadership skills are needed. Styles and skills that may have worked in stable, predictable environments are no longer adequate.

But what are the critical competencies needed by leaders in today's organizations? First and foremost, today's leaders must be able to handle complex adaptive systems (Mathews, White, and Long, 1999) and be able to work in chaos (Wheatley, 1992). Organizations want leaders who have strong interpersonal and communication skills as well as the ability to solve problems and take action. They seek leaders who have the ability to create opportunities and learn from failures. Leaders need to be able to define the problem and understand the environment before attempting to engineer a solution. Collins (2001), in his best-selling classic *From Good to Great,* discovered that leaders of great companies are both humble and persistent.

Vaill (1996) points out the need for today's managers to have a high aptitude for both action and reflection. He notes that self-awareness and astute understanding of one's personal motives is the most critical of all leadership skills. Equipping people to become reflective practitioners will help them become better leaders. Schön (1983) and Argyris (1982) both proclaim the ability to reflect as a key leadership skill. These two authors distinguish between reflection in action (or reflecting while doing) and reflection on action, which is the reviewing that occurs after the event. Unfortunately, rarely do leadership programs focus on the ability to reflect.

Much of the current discussion about leadership revolves around emotional intelligence (EQ), which has been popularized by Goleman (1996, 2000) and others. EQ is seen as an excellent indicator of leadership ability, and unlike IQ, EQ can be improved and developed. Emotional intelligence consists of five primary abilities:

1. *Self-awareness:* the ability to observe oneself and recognize the feeling as it happens
2. *Managing emotions:* the ability to handle feelings so that they are appropriate; realizing what is behind a feeling; finding ways to handle fears and anxieties, anger, and sadness
3. *Motivating oneself:* the ability to channel emotions in the service of a goal; emotional self-control; delaying gratification and stifling impulses
4. *Empathy:* sensitivity to others' feelings and concerns and taking their perspective; appreciating the differences in how people feel about things
5. *Handling relationships:* the ability to manage the emotions in others; this competence includes social competence and social skills

The remarkable strength of action learning is that every leadership skill mentioned above can be demonstrated and utilized in the action learning setting. Situations in which individuals work on real problems and develop accountable strategies with a group of people over whom they have no authority provide the opportunity of practicing all the leadership competencies desired by top management. The most effective way to gain insight into one's leadership style is while under pressure in an unstructured, ill-defined, timed situation (Mumford, 1995). Adding reflective inquiry and shared learning further accentuates the opportunities for increasing the awareness of and competency in leadership.

Action Learning Versus Other Leadership Development Programs

Action learning differs from normal leadership development programs in that it requires members to ask appropriate questions in conditions of risk, rather than to find answers that have already been defined by others—and that do not allow for ambiguous responses because the examiners have all the approved answers (Revans, 1982b). Dilworth (1998) notes that leadership development, as practiced by most organizations, "produces individuals who are technologically literate and able to deal with intricate problem-solving models, but are essentially distanced from the human dimensions that must be taken into account. Leaders thus may become good at downsizing and corporate restructuring, but cannot deal with a demoralized workforce and the resulting longer-term challenges" (p. 49).

The limitation of most management development programs is that they typically focus on a single dimension, unlike action learning, which derives its power from the fact that it does not isolate any dimension from the context in which the managers work; rather, it develops the whole leader for the whole organization. What leaders learn and how they learn cannot be dissociated from one another, for how one learns necessarily influences what one learns.

Most leadership development programs occur away from the organizational environment, and participants work on case studies that offer more information than real-world cases. If individuals make mistakes, there are no real consequences. Also, fellow learners are relative strangers who have limited stake and commitment to provide honest and frank feedback.

Bass (1985) points out that changes in attitudes, assumptions, and values require reflection on the leader's own mental models. Without a change in these models, it is impossible for a leader to change. Densten and Gray (2001) assert that reflection assists the development of leaders by enabling them to gain insight and to take into account the complexities of situations. The habit of seeking insight is the basis for the ability to retool the most basic element of leadership development, that is, ourselves. An important factor in any difficult decision is the character of the manager who makes it; since all managers are unique, development of the individual cannot be taught but must be learned, which is a unique strength of action learning (McNulty and Canty, 1995).

Only through the reflective inquiries of the coach are one's limitations explored. Normally, we do not want to discuss limitations, and thus they are not addressed and do not change. But if people enter the session with the expectation that they need to grow, they can diminish their blind spots and enhance their leadership capacities. In action learning, there are many opportunities for self-reflection as well as supportive feedback from peers who are committed to helping us develop. Everyone is available to help each other develop a "team of leaders."

Learning cannot be solely the acquisition of programmed knowledge. Managers also need to improve their abilities to search out the unfamiliar. Action learning is the Aristotelian manifestation of all managers' jobs: they learn as they lead, and they can lead because they have learned—and go on learning. Dilworth (1998) notes that action learning provides managers with the opportunity to take "appropriate levels of responsibility in discovering how to develop themselves" (p. 37).

Mumford (1995) believes action learning is effective in developing leaders because it incorporates these key elements in management development: learning occurs more as a result of taking action than merely diagnosing and analyzing or recommending action, as most leadership development programs do; working on significant meaningful projects of the managers themselves creates greater learning; and managers learn better from one another than from instructors who are not managers or who have never managed.

Team Learning

Action learning quickly forges groups into high-performing work teams who are able to think, create, act, and learn as a powerful entity. Unlike most groups that begin and often remain at a low level of productivity, action learning groups improve their level of teamwork as well as their team thinking and team learning every time they meet. The team growth commences at the first meeting, when members are advised of the importance of learning as a team, a necessity for the group to become smarter and better able to successfully and innovatively solve the problem or problems they must overcome as a team.

Earlier we identified eight ingredients of a successful, high-performance work group. Let's briefly analyze how action learning creates and reinforces those features.

Shared commitment to solving problem. In action learning, the group is formed to accomplish a specific purpose, namely, to solve a particular problem. The members realize that they are accountable and that they must work together if they are going to be successful.

Building a Team of Leaders at a Global Management Consulting Firm

Chuck Appleby, Executive Director, Great Enterprise Consortium

Rapid growth in the information assurance business created an unprecedented need for development of key leadership skills in a major management consulting firm. Top management sought a high-impact development methodology and chose action learning. Eight newly promoted managers were selected for a pilot action learning program that included eight sessions over a six-month period, with one-on-one coaching during the intervals between the meetings. Each meeting focused on the challenge of one of the eight members. The sessions also included discussion of supplementary leadership issues that were identified through feedback from customers and other managers.

Participants and top management were very pleased with the program and believed that action learning had indeed made a difference. The eight participants described the benefits of action learning not just in terms of the development of innovative solutions, but in the power of peer pressure in ensuring that they implemented the strategies developed by the group. The in-between coaching sessions helped them to explore and reflect further on some of the difficult issues raised in the sessions. Everyone felt that action learning created a supportive peer network. Top management in the firm noted significant improvement in participant performance in leading, working in teams, and solving problems.

Clear and common goal. In action learning, the team never assumes that there is clear agreement on the goal for the group, and thus the first step is to jointly clarify the goal and achieve agreement on the group's purpose. Members realize that consensus on a goal is possible only if they ask questions of each other. To confirm the consensus, the action learning coach will check with the group regularly before allowing them to begin working on solutions.

Willingness to work with others to develop strategies. In action learning, the group members often are thrust into problems and situations entirely new to them, as the organization has sought individuals who may have fresh questions in addition to individuals who have experience with the issue. Thus, no one in the group has all the information, resources, or political power necessary to solve the problem. Everyone's perspectives, knowledge, and experience are needed to understand the issues and develop possible strategies.

Courage to question others. In action learning, everyone is expected, even required, to ask questions of each other. No one has all the answers, and asking fresh questions is critical for the group's ultimate success. Taking risks is one of the skills developed in this setting.

Clear and accepted norms. Action learning groups are presented with particular rules, or norms: reflective inquiry, questions before statements, commitment to learning, confidentiality, focusing on problem solving and taking action, and having an action learning coach. The unique norms of each group are then established through the reflections and agreements made during the sessions, primarily at the first meeting. These norms are powerfully established within action learning groups and are thus rarely violated.

Respecting others and supporting their ideas. As a result of the interplay of the six components of action learning, particularly as members share their learnings and vulnerabilities through the interventions of the coach, action learning groups generate a positive and healthy regard for one another.

Willingness to learn and help others to learn. When action learning groups begin, members are reminded that the group has two purposes, namely, to work on the issue and to learn. Throughout the program, time and energy will be spent on learning about the self, the team, and the organization. Accepting the responsibility to learn and to help others learn generates a helping and sensitive atmosphere within the group.

Cohesiveness and trust. A strong bond is built in action learning groups as members jointly focus on reframing problems and developing strategies. Interconnectedness is also built by the egalitarian nature of the groups, in which the quality of questions rather than the ability to provide answers is important. Finally, high levels of trust are built when people share their vulnerabilities.

Team and Organizational Learning at GE

General Electric has utilized action learning perhaps longer than any other American company. Action learning has enabled GE people to learn and apply new skills while working on real problems—skills such as team building, conflict resolution, problem solving, coaching and facilitating, and understanding change management methodologies and tools, as well as communication methodologies. Over the past twenty years, GE has used action learning to help it become a learning organization in which the following results have been achieved.

▲ Boundaryless behavior in which employees work more easily across borders and business units
▲ Greater speed in decision making and implementation
▲ Accountability at appropriate levels with less controlling leadership
▲ Involvement of employees and resulting improved morale
▲ A management willing to take more risks
▲ Reduction of the culture of analysis paralysis
▲ More open dialogue and increased trust among staff
▲ Reduced impact of the burdens of hierarchy ■

Organizational Learning

Action learning is perhaps the quickest and most effective means of building a learning organization. Action learning groups model learning organizations because learning is a continuous, strategically used process that is integrated with, and runs parallel to, the work of the group. In order to survive, organizations, like action learning groups, must be able to continuously adapt, renew, and revitalize themselves in response to the rapidly changing environment. Learning organizations seek to learn faster and more efficiently from failures as well as successes. Zuboff (1988) notes that productivity and learning in the workplace are becoming one and the same, that "learning is the new form of labor" (p. 395).

A learning organization is constructed around four primary components: increased learning skills and capacities, a transformed organizational culture and structure, an involvement of the entire business chain in the learning process, and enhanced capability to manage knowledge (Marquardt, 2002). Members of action learning groups transfer their experiences and new capabilities to the organization to build these four components.

Increased Learning Skills and Capacities
Within the action learning process, the group members develop their metacognition skills, that is, their ability to learn. They learn the principles and theories of effective learning, the ways in which learning can be augmented and applied, the different types of learning (anticipatory, adaptive, generative), as well as the key skills of learning (testing personal mastery, understanding mental models, systems thinking). In action learning individuals learn how to learn as a team, an opportu-

nity made possible by the reflective questions of the action learning coach. Finally, the action learning process enables people to discover and experience how organizational learning occurs through the shared insights, knowledge, and mental models of members of the organization and by building on the past knowledge and experience of the organization (i.e., policies, strategies, explicit models).

Transformed Organizational Culture and Structure

Action learning develops values important for the culture of a learning organization, a culture in which learning is seen as essential for corporate success, where learning becomes a natural part of all organizational functions. Members of action learning groups come from all levels and units of the organization, thus enabling them to work more comfortably and confidently with groups from across organizational departments and functions. Strategies are used that build the learning capacities of its members. Learning organizations operate with minimal hierarchies, structures, and bureaucracies. Like action learning groups, they are fluid, flexible, and streamlined, and they maximize communication flow and innovative action.

Involvement of the Entire Business Chain in the Learning Process

Learning organizations involve not only staff in the learning process, but also customers, suppliers, vendors, and even the community. Organizational learning requires that we examine the organizational system as a whole. In action learning, members are always on the lookout for people both within and outside the organization who may possess the knowledge, power, or passion necessary to successfully reframe the problem, develop strategies, and take action. Gaining the perspectives and wisdom of fresh faces opens up the boundaries of possible learnings and actions.

Enhanced Capability to Manage Knowledge

Action learning models and allows members to practice and apply each of the aspects of knowledge management.

> *Acquiring knowledge.* In action learning sets, members recognize not only the importance of acquiring information from external resources, but also the value of tapping the tacit, internal wisdom and experience of each other. The internal networks developed in action learning sets heighten the awareness of organizational resources, facilitate exchanging and sharing of ideas, and generate new knowledge.

Creating knowledge. Nonaka (1994) suggests that information creation is a fundamental requirement for the self-renewing (i.e., learning) organization. Participants in action learning programs understand that they should seek new ways of solving old problems, that the old knowledge may no longer be sufficient. Thus, members are constantly searching for novel strategies, taking risks in a supportive setting, pilot testing alternative solutions, and so on.

Storing knowledge. Knowledge needs to be categorized and stored according to learning needs, work objectives, user expertise, and function so that it can be found quickly and accurately. Through their ongoing reflection on learning and the knowledge acquired, action learning groups develop the ability to make meaning of the data collected and to store it within the group's memory or in the organization as appropriate. The action learning coach regularly checks out what knowledge is being stored and why.

Transferring and testing knowledge. Action learning groups continuously seek ways in which they can transfer the learnings, wisdom, and experience gained within the group to the organizations and communities in which they work. The knowledge is tested by determining whether it does indeed work.

Why Action Learning Generates Powerful and Relevant Learning

Learning is so rich and relevant in action learning groups because the process incorporates a wide array of important adult learning principles and practices, and it selects from and integrates the theories from all five schools of learning.

Incorporation of Adult Learning Principles

Adult education specialists over the past century have identified a number of principles and practices that increase the speed, understanding, quality, and application of learning, particularly for the workplace. Action learning builds upon each of them, specifically the following fourteen principles.

▲ Adults are motivated to learn as they experience needs and interests that learning will satisfy.
▲ We learn not so much when we are motivated to learn, but when we are motivated to achieve something.

Action Learning and Knowledge Harvesting at British Airport Authority

British Airport Authority (BAA) is the world's largest airports operator, with a dominant UK position and global programs in the United States (Pittsburgh, Indianapolis) and in Melbourne. Action learning was introduced in the 1980s as part of a knowledge-creating and -sharing culture called Project Harvest. Some fifty managers were involved in five different projects. With the first wave of managers, more than two hundred new items of knowledge were generated from tackling real business challenges, including the forecasting at Southampton airport and managing the construction of Heathrow express rail service.

As a part of the action learning program, there were concentrated efforts to augment learning by encouraging action learning groups to cascade knowledge gained to those around them, with a special focus on program outcomes and their effects on profit and loss with the enterprise. The real challenge was to share this knowledge with those others within the organization who could act upon it in their own roles and in response to their own challenges. A comprehensive database was created, an important part, but only a part, of the answer to knowledge management. Key benefits of the action learning were the macro-level analysis and dissemination of the knowledge to achieve Project Harvest. (Christie and Sandelands, 2000)

▲ Experience is the richest resource for adults' learning, and thus the core methodology of adult education is the analysis of experience.

▲ Learning intensifies when we reflect on what we have experienced; and the more recent the experience we reflect on, the greater and more intense the learning.

▲ Learning is deepest when it involves the whole person, mind, values, and emotions.

▲ We learn more when we are responsible and accountable for applying the learning.

▲ Significant learning occurs when one is forced to sort through the past for relevant concepts, put ideas together in unique ways, and seek new information.

▲ Learning increases when we are asked questions or ask questions of ourselves.

▲ The strongest learning occurs when there is both an urgency and sufficient time and space to deal with the urgency.

▲ Critical, transformative learning occurs when we are able to question our assumptions.

▲ We learn when we receive accurate feedback from others and we are encouraged and supported in our deliberations.

▲ Group responsibility for learning empowers members and enhances learning of the entire group.

▲ Working on unfamiliar problems in unfamiliar settings causes us to unfreeze some of our previous ways of doing things and develop powerful learnings since we are faced with challenges and difficulties that are difficult to address.

▲ We learn best when we can see results and are allowed to take risks.

Integration of Best Theories from Five Schools of Learning

Action learning utilizes the theories, principles, and practices of each of the five schools of adult learning, namely, the cognitive, behavioral, social, humanist, and constructivist learning schools. Unlike most training programs that tend to follow one approach or another to learning, action learning bridges the schools and consequently builds a uniquely powerful learning opportunity for individuals, teams, and organizations. Let's examine how action learning applies the best practices of each of the five schools.

Cognitive Learning

Cognitive learning theorists (Bruner, Argyris, Schön, and Piaget, among others) are concerned primarily with how the brain processes information and experience, and then converts it into knowledge, skills, and values. Action learning incorporates key elements of cognitive psychology through its focus on metacognition skills and learning how to learn; the internal process of acquiring and retaining information; using the problem as a trigger for the internal mental process of learning; looking for patterns, insights, and understandings while reflecting; and thinking about doing while doing.

Behavioral Learning

Behavioralists such as Skinner and Tolman believe that creating the proper environment and stimuli will create the ideal conditions for maximizing learning or any other behaviors. In action learning, the strong stimuli are the urgent, critical problem that needs to be resolved and the pressure on the group to develop effective solutions as well as to improve individual, team, and organizational behaviors. There is also pressure from the group and the coach to observe the norms. A specific group size (four to eight members) provides the optimum number for decision making and the active involvement of all members. Group members are required to ask questions, which causes synapses to be open and prevents domination of any individual. The action learning coach also causes behavior modification through her interventions.

Social Learning

Social learning theorists such as Dewey, Bandura, Lave, and Wenger emphasize the social nature of learning, the importance of the context or environment in which learning occurs and that causes learning to occur. For them, learning requires social interaction and collaboration. Learners seek to connect past and present experiences, and learning is facilitated through "communities of practice," a social context in which action and learning are important. An effective way to learn is through modeling competencies, skills, and learning. The individual makes sense of an experience by conceptualizing it and generalizing the replicable points, and plans for future actions based on the learning gathered. The group provides the forge in which an individual's actions are shaped through contemplation and the insightful questioning of fellow group members.

Humanist Learning

Humanists (Rogers, Maslow, Knowles, and others) believe that everyone has untapped abilities to contribute, to learn, and to act. Learning requires support and caring among fellow group members, so there is a comfort and freedom for asking fresh questions. Learning to seek what is unique to each situation as well as what is significant for each individual is an essential element of humanist learning theory. This school also emphasizes that the best learning occurs when the whole person (affective, cognitive, psychomotor dimensions) is involved. Everyone is responsible for his own as well as others' learnings. Creativity and innovation are encouraged. Each of these principles is inherent in action learning.

Constructivist Learning

For constructivist learning theorists such as Weick, Vgotsky, Illich, Friere, and Mezirow, knowledge and learning are context bound. Individuals and groups construct learning, as well as norms and meaning, from the action or experience. Being forced to deal with an unfamiliar problem or setting generates transformative learning and innovation.

People need to inquire of each other's perspectives. Constructivists posit that learning optimally occurs by the interaction with the environment in a problem-anchored and learner-centered approach. Action learning's focus on learning with real problems with real applications thus incorporates the key elements of constructivist learning theories.

Learning from Experience

B. F. Skinner, a leading proponent of behavioralism and behavioral learning, stated that the "major difference between rats and people is that rats learn from experience." Most of us are members of groups that never seem to improve in their efficiency or effectiveness. Staff meetings are a prime example. How many of our staff meetings ever improve? Are they any better than they were six months ago or six years ago? Yet we continue to attend them. A rat attends a bad meeting only one time, and then it stops attending. Humans keep on returning—we don't learn from experience. In Johnson and Blanchard's (1998) bestseller *Who Moved My Cheese?* the mice in the story move to other parts of the land when the cheese is finished at one site, whereas the humans keep returning to the same place, expecting the cheese to somehow magically reappear. The mice learn from experience. ■

Intensity and Power of the Action Learning Experience

Wilfred Bion (1991), a noted British psychologist, observed that individuals, teams, and organizations could and, in fact, did have the ability to change their behavior quickly and permanently when faced with an *intense experience* to which they responded with the proper *attitude* and *discipline*—for example, a tremendous external environmental threat, the birth of a child (for parents), or surviving on an island (for a group). Action learning does, in fact, provide that *intensity* (a problem, comrades in adversity who need to hang together or hang separately, the requirement to take action with no certainty of success, with people who may be unfamiliar to us or to the problem); that *attitude* (working as a team, the need to learn, seeking innovation and success); and that *discipline* (statements only in response to questions, listening to each other and the action learning coach, being present at each session).

The most powerful form of learning, the most sophisticated form of staff development, comes not from listening to the good words of others but from sharing what we know with others. Learning comes more from giving than from receiving. By reflecting on what we do, by giving it coherence, and by sharing and articulating our craft, knowledge, we make meaning, we learn.
—Roland Barth (1981)

The Power of Learning in Action Learning

Because action learning is built on and applies so many dynamics of the field of learning, it generates an amazing speed, depth, and breadth of learning.

Speed of learning. In action learning, the participants go through all cycles in a continuous and seamless fashion. The speed of the learning is what enables action learning groups to quickly develop as individuals and as a team.

Depth of learning. Since questions are continuous and challenge one another's assumptions and perspectives, there is significant depth of learning. Reflective questions raised in dialogue create double-loop (reasons why) and triple-loop (systems behind the whys) levels of learnings.

Breadth of learning. Through the guidance of the action learning coach, new learnings and knowledge transfer across teams and organizations.

The potency gained from this learning transforms individuals, teams, and organizations. The resultant power allows for rapid and meaningful success in personal and organizational arenas.

Checklist for Learning

▲ What is the quality of our learnings?

▲ How are we optimizing our learnings?

▲ How is the action learning coach effectively helping us learn?

▲ What questions have been most effective for guiding our reflections and learnings? Why?

▲ Are we growing as individuals? How?

▲ How are we learning as a team? How can we improve ourselves as a team?

▲ Are we interweaving learning and action in the workplace?

▲ Have we transferred knowledge to other parts of the organization? Why or why not?

▲ Are we applying our new skills in the workplace?

▲ In our team, do we have an environment where it is safe to take risks?

▲ How are we learning from our mistakes?

▲ Is our environment one that is collaborative, supportive, and concerned about learning?

▲ Are we taking time to focus on our learning?

▲ Are we questioning our basic assumptions?

▲ Are we taking responsibility as a group for our learning?

▲ Are we learning from reflecting on our experience in the group as well as from actions taken outside the group?

The Coach

The action learning coach is the catalyst that optimizes the power as well as the enjoyment of action learning. She is the synergizer, the glue that bonds group members, and the one who enhances the group's ability to learn and to take vigorous action. The primary role of the coach is to facilitate the group's ability to grow and learn so that it, in turn, can better solve the problem. The focus of the coach must always remain on the learning, not the problem. Learning will provide the leverage for continuously improving group performance.

Through the use of reflective questions, the coach helps group members to examine their actions and interactions and thereby improve their ability as a group to solve the problem as well as future problems they may encounter as a team or as individuals. The more the coach is able to improve the speed and quality of learning and the growth of the group, the more successful the group's work will be. The coach acts as a mirror, enabling the group to reflect on its experience and convert that reflection into learning opportunities and results.

The learning coach models the listening and questioning skills needed by high-performance work groups. Her questions should be open and supportive and should enable the group to reflect on how

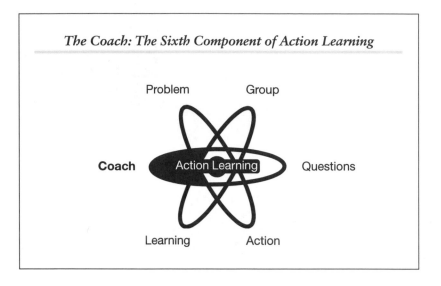

The Coach: The Sixth Component of Action Learning

they are doing as a group, how they can improve, what they are learning, and how their learning can be applied to themselves and to their organizations. Her enthusiasm for learning and her commitment to helping the group succeed should be evident to the group.

Why Is One Person Designated to Focus on the Learning?

Although it certainly would be possible for any group member to focus on the learning and to ask the questions assigned to the action learning coach, the reality is that these tasks are rarely performed unless someone is designated to concentrate on them. In the absence of a designated action learning coach, the reflective learning questions are simply not asked or are not of good quality and timing.

To maximize individual and group learning, one person must be designated to focus exclusively on that task. Problem solvers (i.e., the group members) are focused, as they should be, on the *urgent* problem. The urgency of the problem always overwhelms the importance of learning. Thus, a person who has power must be assigned this important role, or else it gets lost because of time pressure (the tyranny of the urgent).

Action learning is dependent on a few simple rules and processes. The action learning coach ensures that these are followed. Unless he is empowered to see that the group takes time to learn, there is no one who makes sure that sufficient time is set aside for capturing learning. The coach creates and promotes the atmosphere of learning and reflective inquiry. It is simply too much to expect anyone to manage the learning as well as the problem.

If no one is assigned the role of coach and everyone becomes responsible for it, the learning questions will either be asked too often in too many ways or not at all. And the questions will probably be asked for purposes other than to help the group learn. In addition, group members may resent or may be uncomfortable with anyone in the group at any time arbitrarily assuming the role and functions of the action learning coach. Taking over this responsibility in a spontaneous way will likely be challenged.

Who Serves As Action Learning Coach?

The role and responsibilities of the action learning coach may either be rotated among the group members or be filled by an external person who serves as the coach for the life of the group. If the coach is a group member, the role will probably rotate within the group. Thus, at each session or for each problem presenter (multiple groups), a different person would serve as the coach. There are a number of benefits to rotating the role of coach:

▲ Everyone in the group develops this leadership competency of helping people learn and develop.
▲ Serving as an action learning coach enables members to understand the value and appreciate the importance of the coaching role when they return to working on the problem.
▲ While serving as the coach, each person develops new skills in asking solid, learning-inducing questions.
▲ The group or organization saves the time and cost of an outsider.
▲ Confidentiality becomes less of an issue if the content of the problem and solutions must remain only with the select group working on the problem.
▲ The coach usually sees options and insights not apparent to others in the group who are involved with the details of solving the problem; this helicopter perspective can then be brought into the group when the coach rejoins as a group member.

There are also benefits in having a permanent external person (whether internal to the organization or an external consultant) act as coach. This option allows all group members to be involved in the problem at each session, and it gives the group a person with experience, expertise, and confidence in the coaching role. A skilled and experienced coach can significantly enhance the quality of action and the learning of the group.

Building the Learning Climate of the Group

The action learning coach helps to set the climate of learning, openness, trust, and nonjudgment. He should demonstrate frank, targeted questioning and reflecting skills. Although he may be tempted to get involved with the problem, he must always focus on the process and interactions and strive to find opportunities for developing the group.

The coach should not be put in the role of being the expert, controller, teacher, or chairperson. However, it is valuable if she is more knowledgeable and experienced in action learning than the other members of the group, as she may be responsible for orienting and preparing group members on the fundamentals of action learning, including the elements and ground rules.

The coach never tells group members what to do, but through questions assists them in discovering what they need to do. She does not teach, but seeks to create an atmosphere wherein members can learn for and from themselves, develop confidence in themselves, reflect, and develop new ideas (Lawlor, 1997). The role of the coach is not to correct or to be critical, but rather to raise the group's consciousness about what is happening.

The coach must always be cognizant of the fact that significant learning occurs as a result of getting the group to reflect, and significant reflection occurs as a result of good questions. He must also help the group members to assume responsibility for learning and for taking their knowledge and learning back to other parts of their lives. He initiates all of these essential processes through questions—the right ones at the right time.

Questions: The Modus Operandi of the Coach

The action learning coach only asks questions, unless he is asked a question by the group. Why is it so important for the coach to only ask questions? First, questions cause people to reflect and therefore to learn. If the primary role of the coach is to get people to reflect and learn, then it is appropriate that he do this through questioning. In action learning, we expect group members to ask questions, and to make statements only in response to questions; therefore it is important that the coach model the behavior that he expects from the group.

Questions are always more powerful and valuable than statements if you want an individual or a group to consider a perspective other than its own. Also, statements from the coach, unlike questions, will cause people to become defensive, defiant, and/or dependent on the coach; all these reactions are contrary to the spirit and power of action learning. If this occurs, the coach will be seen as unobjective, insensitive, controlling, or manipulative.

The coach should not be seen as taking sides on issues or making judgments about the behavior or attitude of group members. Good reflective questions are nonjudgmental. The person responding will make his own judgments. Thus the members need not be afraid that the coach will be jumping in and pointing out an idea or behavior that may have been detrimental to the group or indicative of a negative personality trait.

A final reason why it is best for the coach to ask questions is that it allows the group to reflect and make their own decisions. For example, if the coach perceives an action as being negative or positive, and makes a statement to that effect, then the group may accept his statement as the truth, even if that judgment is incorrect. As a result, the group may be totally misdirected in its work and its learnings.

The Power of the Coach to Intervene

The second ground rule of action learning is that the coach has the power to intervene when she sees fit; and when she does intervene, the group needs to stop working on the problem and listen to the question or questions raised by the coach. The group should continue focusing on the coach's questions until she leans back and indicates to the group that it may resume working on the problem. Likewise, after sufficient forewarning as to the closing time for working on the problem, the coach has the power to end the problem-solving phase of the session so that she has sufficient time to assist the group in capturing and applying its learnings.

It is critical that the group devote a portion of its time to learning, yet we know from our experience that, without an intervening mechanism, the importance of learning will be overshadowed by the urgency of the problem. Therefore, power must be given to the person in charge of what is important so that he can overrule the natural tendency to go with the power of what is urgent.

If time for reflection and learning is not guaranteed when the coach requests it, then it simply will not happen. Experience and research show that this aspect of group work is abandoned unless it is the chief and sole responsibility of a designated person. The coach must be given this power, particularly if he is seen as a lower-level person in the organization. If he is perceived as someone with less knowledge or experience on the problem, he will be ignored and/or overruled by other members of the group unless he is specifically given this authority.

Therefore, when the coach leans forward and joins the circle, the group immediately stops (or completes the sentence or thought begun) and listens to the questions of the action learning coach. As long as she is within the work circle, she has control of the discussion. It is important that she not lose that control and allow the group to jump back into the problem before she has indicated that members may resume, for once a group ignores the coach, it will be difficult to regain that authority in future interventions. If she can successfully and comfortably retain control during the first intervention, she will be more easily able to retain it for the rest of the life of that group.

Should the Coach Be Involved in Problem Solving?

Although there are times when the coach would like to focus on the problem because of an idea or insight he may have, in general this is discouraged for several reasons.

> *Loss of objectivity and fairness.* If the coach becomes involved in the discussion, his viewpoint may be seen as being supportive of one group member or another. Then, when reflective questions are asked by the coach at the end of the session, the people who feel slighted might not see the coach or his questions as being objective or open or fair. As a result, their reflections or responses may not be valuable to the group's growth or group members may be uncomfortable with each other.
>
> *Problem is seen as more important than the learning.* In action learning, we place so much importance on learning that we designate an individual to focus her entire attention on it. If the coach becomes involved in the action, she is indicating to the group that the problem is more important than the learning. It becomes diffi-

cult later to recapture the sense that the coach truly believes the learning is so important that it needs her entire attention.

Coach is unable to focus on learning. If the action learning coach is involved in the problem, he may not be focusing on preparing questions to ask or on the best timing for his intervention. If the appropriate time to intervene is right after he has asked a problem-related question or answered another person's question, his intervention may be seen as self-serving and an opportunity to break up the problem solving when his ideas are inserted.

Imbalance of power or expertise. Because the action learning coach has been granted authority when intervening on issues of learning, she has an aura of power and expertise that may unduly influence the decision making and participation of other members of the group. Her participation in the problem solving may become overweighted, or decisions may be made in deference to her.

Loss of coaching power. If the coach becomes involved, his power may dwindle as he uses more and more airtime. He will tend to lose the credibility and neutrality he should have while serving as the learning coach.

Lack of confidence in the group. If the coach feels that unless she intervenes the group will miss an important insight or solution, she is indicating to group members that she does not trust them, that they need her to save them. The group will become either more dependent or more resentful as time goes on.

Of course, there may be situations and occasions when the learning coach does involve herself in the problem, for example, when the group has only three or four members and the diversity value of the coach is needed. However, she should become involved with caution and be fully aware of the potentially negative consequences of her interventions.

Facilitating Versus Coaching

In action learning, we make a distinction between the role and actions of a coach and those of a group facilitator. Although there is certainly much overlap between these two roles, there are also clear differences in terms of emphasis and philosophical beliefs. To illustrate some of the differences, let us briefly examine the two roles. Table 5 summarizes these differences.

Table 5	*Facilitator's Role Versus Learning Coach's Role*

Facilitator	Learning Coach
Focus on group process	Focus on learning and improving team
• Team norms	• Performance and actions
• Decision making	• Making learning explicit
• Communications and feedback	
Statements	Reflective questions
What happened	Why and how happened
• Focused on desired outcomes	• Aligning intentions and action
Dependence	Independence
Single-loop learning	Double-loop and triple-loop learning
	• Connecting learning to business
	• Skills of learning
Focus on the present/past	Focus on the future/present
Builds fear and threatening relationship	Builds comforting and trusting relationship
Focus on the *what*	Focus on the *why*
Generates reaction	Generates reflection
Depends on expertise	Depends on perspective
Values cleverness	Values wisdom
Offers answers	Generates more questions and insights
Generates dependent thinking	Fosters critical thinking
People grow in manner desired by facilitator	People grow into the future they desire
Beliefs and behavior misaligned	Alignment of behavior and beliefs

The facilitator's primary role is to help the group improve its functioning. He does this by observing and occasionally making statements and offering advice on what the group could do better. This is expected from the group, since this person has been trained to be a facilitator and that is his role. The members depend on him to guide them, and they hope that their individual behaviors, if not productive, are not publicized or blown out of proportion by the facilitator. The expertise and role of the facilitator can lead to dependence and, in some cases, resentment.

The primary role of the action learning coach is to enable the members to take responsibility for themselves to learn how to develop as a team, to increase their awareness of how they are doing, and to generate norms and processes that will improve their effectiveness. The focus is on learning and connecting that learning to action, and the means to achieve that learning is reflective questioning. Action learning groups become increasingly confident in their own internal ability to manage their group process and to successfully complete their tasks. The role of the coach needs to be performed by someone, but any of us would be able to do it if called upon. Group members do not need to worry about being judged or criticized by the coach. The values of action learning are perfectly embodied in the coach. Members quickly become very comfortable with the coach and with each other. The process becomes ever more seamless and natural.

Motivating Versus Empowering

An important nuance in implementing the role of the action learning coaching is understanding the distinction between motivating and empowering the group. Motivation relies on the external, whereas empowerment believes in the internal capacity of people. The action learning coach seeks to empower whenever and in whatever way she can. She believes that each and every member is needed and can contribute to the group. The group and its members have a variety of internal capabilities and talents. People can and should discover what they must change and learn, and should be held accountable for their decisions and actions. Internal expectations and fulfillment rather than external threats or rewards should be what stimulate and inspire them. Table 6 summarizes the distinctions between the motivating and empowering approaches.

Interventions and Questions

In addition to knowing what questions to ask and how to ask questions, knowing *when* to intervene is an important skill for the action learning coach. Interventions should occur at the *beginning* of each session, one or more times *during* the session, and at the *end* of the action learning session. Let's briefly examine how the action learning coach

Table 6 *Motivating Versus Empowering*

Assumptions for Motivating	Assumptions for Empowering
Something is wrong with people	People need new perspectives; the solution is within
People need to be told what to do	People can learn and change in action
People need to be threatened or rewarded	People need to be held accountable
People need to be comforted	People need appreciation and respect

intervenes at each of these stages and the types of questions he asks during those interventions.

Intervention and Questions at the Beginning of the Session

The coach's first intervention (although technically not an intervention since it occurs before the group begins its work) occurs at the very beginning of the first session of the group. At this time, the coach checks that all the group members are familiar with the principles and norms of action learning. Once he has been assured that the members understand the action learning process, the coach asks the problem presenter(s) to state the problem/challenge. In subsequent meetings of the group, he will ask the individual (in the case of multiple-problem sets) or the group (in single-problem sets) what actions have been taken since the previous session of the group and what has been the impact of those actions as well as learnings gained. Following are examples of questions the coach might ask at the beginning of a session.

▲ Is everyone familiar with how action learning works? With the role of the action learning coach? The importance of questions first?
▲ At first session of multiple-problem set (addressed to the problem presenter): What is the problem (task, challenge, issue) that you would like the group to help you with? Could you take a few minutes to briefly summarize the key elements of the problem?
▲ At first session of single-problem set (addressed to entire group): What is the problem as we understand it?

▲ At subsequent sessions: What actions have been taken since our last session? What has been the impact of those actions? What actions did not occur? Why not? What can we learn from these experiences? What would we do differently? What learnings can be applied to this project? To other parts of our lives or of the organization? How can we transfer these learnings?

Interventions and Questions During the Session

There is no set point at which the coach makes his interventions during sessions. He may sometimes intervene within the first few minutes and at other times not until twenty or even forty minutes have elapsed. He may intervene as many as four to six times during a session or as few as one or two times. He should always intervene at least once, for, in addition to providing the group with some breathing space, it helps members to become more aware of what they are doing well and what they might do better to identify and continue their positive interactions, and to improve upon the obstructive and unproductive behaviors.

There are always some more comfortable and natural times to intervene, for example, when the group is not working well or there is struggling or uncertainty as to what to do next. Enabling the group to be more conscious of the factors that may be causing the difficulty will allow them to address it directly and intentionally and thereby identify actions to remedy or overcome it.

An interesting phenomenon occurs while the coach has the group reflecting on the quality of the group process. While the group consciously works on what it is doing well, what can be improved, and so forth, it subconsciously continues to work on the problem. After the group has finished working on the process, it returns refreshed and invigorated and ready to work on the problem. Amazingly, instead of being sidelined and delayed by the coach's intervention, the group discovers that its subconscious has been thinking about the problem and now generates ideas and solutions that might never have occurred if the group had continued focusing only on the problem.

A wide variety of questions may be asked during the action learning sessions. Generally, they will fall into four major categories: problem framing questions, action strategy questions, group effectiveness questions, and learning questions.

The first question that is normally asked by the action learning coach during a session is, "How are we doing as a team—okay or not okay?" This is an excellent question that allows an easy transition from the intensity of working on the problem to beginning to reflect on the group's process and productivity. Remember that it is difficult for people to move from the urgent problem into a reflective stage in which the focus is on the process and the learning. It is important to obtain everyone's response to this question so that one or a few people's opinions do not determine what the whole group feels or thinks. This question provides an opportunity to get everyone involved, especially the quiet person who may have said little or nothing thus far. This is referred to as a "gut question" because the coach is exploring people's feelings about the quality of the group work to this point.

Once the coach has a sense of how each member feels about the group, he moves from the emotional level to the cognitive or intellectual level by asking the second question, "What have we done well thus far?" Even if everyone answered the first question by saying "not okay," the coach knows that the group has done some things well. For example, at a minimum, everyone is asking questions because of the ground rule, but people are also probably listening, gathering information, and working on the problem. The coach wants the group to identify those positive behaviors so that they continue. In this way, the coach is applying the positive focus of appreciative inquiry (Cooperrider, Sorensen, and Yaeger, 2001), which energizes the group and causes people to be more satisfied and confident when they resume work on the problem.

The coach's next question, "What could we do better?" is also always asked, even if everyone said the group was doing well, because, again, the coach knows that every group has some behaviors that can be improved. The responses to these two questions—"What have we done well?" and "What could we do better?"—begin to form powerful and positive norms that enable the group to immediately improve the manner in which it operates. The group is thus able to avoid the traditional forming-storming-norming-performing pattern and move to the much preferred forming-performing-norming-performing pattern that occurs in action learning groups (see Chapter 3 for a discussion of these stages).

Note the use of the word *we* by the coach when she is asking the questions. This conveys to the group that she is a full member of the group and anxious for its success, even though her role is to focus on a complementary element of the group's work. If the coach instead asked "How are you doing?" she would imply that she is separate from, maybe even above, the group and thus able to avoid responsibility for any failures or weaknesses of the group.

There are many possible questions the coach can ask to help the group ask better questions, listen more carefully, and become more creative. Questions about the quality of the group's questions is important, since the quality of the questions will ultimately determine the success of the group (see Chapter 4). Following are examples of the types of questions frequently asked by coaches during action learning situations.

▲ How are we doing as a team—okay or not okay?
▲ What are we doing well? Can you give an example of what we have done well? What was the impact of that?
▲ What could we do better? Can you be specific?
▲ Do we have clarity and agreement on the problem? (Ask everyone to write it down.)
▲ What is the quality of our questions?
▲ Are we building on each other's questions and ideas? Examples?
▲ What is the balance between questions and statements?
▲ What is the group attempting to accomplish?
▲ Could you turn that into a question?
▲ How creative have we been? How could we be more creative?
▲ (To the problem presenter) What questions have been the most helpful?
▲ What is the quality of our ideas? Our strategies?
▲ Any learnings thus far about the problem content? Leadership? Teams?

The action learning coach should keep the time consumed by his interventions to no more than five to ten minutes so that the group can quickly return to working on the problem. Some interventions may last for a minute, as they consist of one question addressed to one person (e.g., "Jim, what do you think is the impact of your question [or statement] on the group?"). The coach therefore must carefully consider and choose questions that best enable the group to improve its capacity as a group and thereby more quickly and effectively handle the problem the group is working on.

Intervention and Questions at the End of a Session

The intervention and questions at the end of each action learning session provide immensely valuable opportunities for significant and transformative learning for individuals as well as the group. To adequately prepare for the end-of-session intervention, the action learning coach alerts the group about the time frame for the meeting. He might say, for example, "This two-hour session is scheduled to end at 4:00. Since I need the final fifteen minutes to help us capture our learnings and identify ways to apply our knowledge, we will need to complete our work on the problem at 3:45." The coach may then provide a fifteen-minute alert at 3:30 and remind the group to begin focusing on actions that they will be taking between this and the next session. Then at 3:45 the coach moves forward and begins asking questions such as the following. The first set of three questions is always asked to the problem presenter in a multiple-problem set, and to the entire group in a single-problem set.

▲ What actions are you (we) going to take as a result of this session? Were you (we) helped? How?
▲ How did we do as a team? Okay, not okay, great?
▲ What did we do best? What could we do better?
▲ What do we think about the quality of our problem solving? Of our proposed actions?
▲ How could we improve our team and individual efforts?
▲ What helped us make progress? What hindered us?
▲ Which questions were most valuable?
▲ What have we learned about leadership, teamwork, problem solving, company policies, customers, systems thinking (and so on)?
▲ What have you learned about yourself?
▲ How can we apply these learnings to other parts of the organization or to our lives?
▲ What helped us learn?

In multiple-problem sets, each person will have approximately twenty to thirty minutes to receive help and guidance on his or her problem. The coach will tee up each round by letting everyone know the amount of time available for this problem and at what time she will initiate her final intervention. A five-minute reminder may be provided to ensure that action steps are identified before she asks her final questions.

The action learning coach directs the first set of questions to the entire group for single-problem sets or, in multiple-problem sets, to the individual who has just presented the problem. Asking the question "What action are you (we) going to take?" forces the individual or group to articulate specific action steps. No session or subsession should end without a determination and selection of next steps. Being able to respond to this question allows the group some degree of satisfaction that they have indeed helped or begun to help the individual and/or organization. The question "Were you helped?" (which almost always receives an enthusiastic "yes") solidifies the fact that the group has been helpful and valuable. It is rare for an individual or group not to be helped by having questions asked from a variety of perspectives. At a minimum, the problem has become much clearer.

The question "How were you (we) helped?" shows the group how various questions and ideas coalesced and resulted in these useful strategies and possible solutions. It also sets up the group for the second series of questions that focus on how well the group has done, what it has learned, what skills have been developed, and what knowledge can be applied.

The action learning coach needs to choose well which questions will be most valuable and helpful for the group as a whole and for the learning of each individual. Her time will be limited, so she should have selected three or four questions that she believes will accomplish the most learning and provide the greatest leverage for the future.

Intervention and Questions at the End of the Final Meeting

At the last meeting of the group, the coach's intervention is more substantial and may last from thirty minutes to two hours. This is the opportunity to capture the most significant learnings that occurred during the many hours the group deliberated on the problem and implemented actions. The action learning coach facilitates this final session through a systematic exploration of the overall learnings of the group, the most valuable individual learnings, the greatest areas of skill development, the key information and competencies that were or could be transferred to the organization, and the elements and processes that most helped this group to succeed. Following is a list of the types of questions asked at the end of the final meeting.

▲ Did we achieve our goal?
▲ What is the quality of our strategies?
▲ What did we do well? What could we have done better?
▲ What have been your most significant learnings?
▲ What have been the most valuable learnings of the group?
▲ What made us successful?
▲ What did we learn about teams?
▲ Which learnings and skills could be or have been applied to the organization?
▲ What is the quality of our individual development and learning? Of our team development and learning?
▲ Has a systematic analysis of the learning been applied to other parts of the organization?

Follow-up Questions

A script of the beginning, middle, and ending questions listed in this chapter can effectively serve as a guide and starting point for the action learning coach. Valuable and powerful information and change will accrue as the group members respond to these questions. The greatest power and impact, however, generally derives from the follow-up questions raised by the coach. Follow-up questions will quickly elevate the competency level of the group and/or individual. Follow-up questions (sometimes just a "Why?" or "Can you give me an example?" or "How?") create deep levels of learning, transformative learning, and double-loop (causes for) and triple-loop (systems behind) learning. Often a follow-up question simply builds on the response to the previous question. Careful listening is needed for great follow-up questions. Here is a simple illustration of follow-up questioning.

Coach:	What could we do better as a group?
Response:	We could be more creative.
Coach:	How could we be more creative?
Response:	(None)
Coach:	Why do you think we are not being creative?
Response:	I do not think we are building on each other's ideas.
Coach:	Why not?
Response:	Don't know.
Coach:	Anyone else have any thoughts as to why we are not building on each other's ideas?
Response:	I think we are more interested in getting our own ideas into the mix rather than listening to someone else's ideas.
Coach:	Any other ideas as to why we are not building on each other's ideas?
Responses:	(May be several)
Coach:	What is the impact of not being interested in someone else's ideas?
Response:	We show that we do not think much of their ideas.
Coach:	What are some ways in which we could be more creative?

Responses: (May be several)

Coach: Okay, let's resume working on the problem.

As the scenario above illustrates, the coach follows a fairly simple procedure in the asking of follow-up questions. She addresses the first follow-up question to the person who has answered the initial question. After this response, she looks to see if others may have different perspectives and responses or additional comments to the question. If the person addressed does not have a response, the coach quickly turns to the other members of the group for their response(s).

Note that the coach does not have to agree or confirm the response or insight. His responsibility is to help the group become aware of its behavior and the positive or negative consequences of that behavior. Once a group recognizes what is happening and why, it will quickly and almost automatically adapt its behavior to achieve what the group has determined is valuable. In the scenario above, for example, the group, somewhat to its surprise, started asking innovative questions within ten minutes and came up with great strategies by the end of the session. This positive change in the group's interactions occurs naturally and automatically because the coach has helped the group set new norms, and subsequently their desired behaviors are converted into real actions.

> ### Growing Leaders and Coaches at the U.S. Department of Agriculture
>
> The U.S. Department of Agriculture, in its search for an efficient, cost-effective tool to train its leaders in specific leadership competencies, chose action learning. In order to build an internal capacity to continue action learning without contracting for an external action learning coach, the department created a parallel program to develop two internal coaches who were first provided training in action learning coaching and then gradually assumed greater and greater responsibility for the coaching function during the initial two leadership programs. ■

The Art and Skill of Asking Questions

Although inexperienced coaches may initially be concerned about their ability to ask questions, there is generally little to fear since the power is primarily in the question, not in the person asking the question. Using the questions listed in this chapter can provide the starting point. Listening carefully to the response will provide the clues for the follow-up questions. As people gain experience in serving in the role of the action learning coach, the questions flow more easily and they become more relaxed and confident in introducing the next questions.

It is best if the coach phrases her questions positively, using what Cooperrider, Sorensen, and Yaeger (2001) refer to as *appreciative* inquiry. Instead of asking what went wrong, the coach asks questions that focus on what has gone well, what can be done, how it can be improved. The approach will guide the group in seeking what might be rather than what is not. The focus remains on improvement and continuous learning rather than complaining and venting.

It is important and comforting to know that the coach accomplishes much of his objective simply by asking the questions. The subconscious of the group members will wrestle with the coach's questions while working on the problem, and changes will begin to occur simply because the question was asked.

Although the action learning coach is not directly involved in working on the problem, it is important that he show his deep interest in the problem and his sympathetic concern that the group is successful and is working well as a team. He can demonstrate this by body language that communicates his support for the group. It is also helpful for him to jot down notes and possible questions to ask at the time of his intervention. Observe when the energy level of the group is rising and falling. When someone says, "That is a great question!" be sure to write that question down and later ask about it. The key to an eventual innovative solution has its seeds in that question.

Coaches should be comfortable when there is silence or there is no immediate response to a question. Allow group members to reflect and let them know that you are comfortable with the silence. If the person who is asked a question is unable to answer it, after a few seconds ask the question of the rest of the group. Sometimes there will be no response. That is okay, as the question will continue to incubate in people's minds, and a number of responses will emerge when that same question is asked at the next intervention. Remember that the power and value are often more in the question and the reflection that it causes than in the responses that it generates. Also, the coach has prepared the subconscious to reflect on the questions asked during previous interventions, and the next time he asks the same question, the responses will be greater and richer.

The Power of Questions

What makes the questions of the learning coach so powerful? Why do they generate rapid and significant change in the culture and behavior of the group? The intensity of the situation and the quality of the questions produce this effect. Bion (1991) notes that if something is done intensely and well, it needs to occur only once for behavior and values to change. In action learning, group members know that their success depends on each other, that together they are accountable for the solution to the problem. In addition, as they have identified areas for learning and growth, they have shared their vulnerabilities. The magnitude of the context combined with the role and power of the learning coach causes the questions to go to both the consciousness and, even more strongly, the subconsciousness of each member of the group. The resultant responses trigger a natural biological need to change the individual's and the group's behaviors.

It is also valuable to note again that while people are focusing on learnings as a result of questions addressed to them by the coach, their subconscious minds are working on the problem. The reverse behavior occurs once the coach allows the group to return to working on the problem; namely, the subconscious is now working on the learning while the conscious mind is working on the problem.

Reflection, which is critical for the generation of innovative ideas, is made intentional by the coach and results in the interweaving of emotional and cognitive mind-sets. The questions of the coach cause members to return to the experience and replay it. This helps them to capture and acknowledge the feelings associated with the experience.

The Coaching Process Accelerates Learning

A significant amount of research has been undertaken in the past fifty years to identify ways and means to enhance the speed, quality, and retention of learning. Some of the best known and respected research was conducted by Heiman and Slomianko (1990), who identified the four actions that were deemed most critical for increasing the speed and quality of learning. These are:

▲ Asking questions (which cause the synapses to open, which allows the brain to better receive data and learn)
▲ Breaking up complex ideas and tasks into understandable, specific parts

▲ Being asked to identify what and how one has learned
▲ Connecting and applying the learning to specific goals or actions

We can see that all four of these actions are an integral part of action learning. The coach explicitly and purposefully executes each of these actions on a regular basis. Through his questions, he helps to bring to the consciousness of the group what is happening and what people are learning. They become more aware of how they are learning and how they can apply it elsewhere.

Values of the Action Learning Coach

Because of the intensity and intimacy of the action learning process, group members will quickly come to see the attitude of the coach toward them. A positive, humanistic confidence toward people in general will make the coach much more effective and enjoyable to work with. With the right attitude and right questions, the coach becomes highly valued and appreciated by the group. Carter McNamara (2002), a leading action learning theorist and practitioner, recently identified several values and attitudes that the coach should embrace relative to members of action learning groups.

▲ Members have great or even unlimited potential.
▲ They must develop first and primarily from within themselves.
▲ Learning and development include the whole person—thoughts, feelings, head, and heart.
▲ People can develop a great deal by asking the right questions and by closely examining their assumptions and perspectives about themselves and the world around them.
▲ The goals and direction of coaching come from the nature and needs of the group members.
▲ The role of actions and experience are critical to learning and development; without practice, there is no knowledge.
▲ Coaching is a way of working with people that should leave them more competent, more fulfilled, and more able to contribute to their organizations and to find meaning in what they do.

Additional Roles of the Action Learning Coach

In addition to the coaching role that occurs with action learning groups, the coach may be called on to serve a variety of other roles to ensure the success of action learning in the organization.

Trainer/Teacher

Often the action learning coach is responsible for orienting and preparing individuals and the organization as a whole for action learning. She should brief them on the basic principles and benefits of action learning, including the six components and two ground rules. Such training may occur before large groups prior to the establishment of an organization's action learning programs (see Chapter 8 for more details on preparatory workshops). At the beginning of the first learning sessions, the coach introduces or reviews the fundamental components of action learning, particularly her role as the coach.

The teaching role may arise during sessions when the coach is asked by group members to explain why an activity is or is not working, or is asked to offer a technique or tool or concept that might help the group improve the quality or speed of its work. This connecting of current activities to a principle or theory can provide a valuable service to group members. It is important never to impose help but to either respond to a request or to introduce help by asking questions such as "Would a tool be helpful here?" or "What principle or theory is occurring here?"

Administrator

In most organizations, the action learning coach also serves as the administrative coordinator and manager of the action learning program. He is involved in arranging the sites and dates of the sessions and serves as a bridge between the group and top management. He maintains contact with key people outside the groups to ensure their continued support, and he updates appropriate people as necessary. He may need to work with the sponsor to assure him that the group is progressing well or to confirm that he will support the action being proposed by the group. He may serve as a link with and provide support for the organization's action learning champions. Between meetings of the groups, he may send reminders of upcoming sessions, of agreed-upon actions, and of the importance of applying the learnings in other parts of the organization. If the group is composed of people from different organizations, he may need to serve as the key link and contact point among the various organizations.

Adviser/Champion/Internal Marketer/Promoter

Another critical role played by action learning coaches is that of the cheerleader for action learning, the person who promotes action learning to top management and throughout the organization, who develops the appropriate orientation programs and announcements, who recruits sponsors and champions, who advises those affected by the action learning groups. Organizations with several action learning coaches may divide the responsibilities of promoting, championing, and advising.

Skills and Attributes of the Successful Coach

There are a number of important skills, values, and attributes that will enable the action learning coach to be successful. Let's briefly examine each of them.

Ability to Ask Questions

The key skill of the action learning coach is the ability to ask good questions. Her questions should make people think and feel challenged; they should be supportive and positive rather than critical. To ask good questions consistently, the coach needs to have a strong and sincere belief in the power of questions and the critical role of the action learning coach in asking questions. The manner of introducing questions should be gentle and never arrogant. The coach should screen herself and determine whether her question will be truly helpful to the group. She should be looking at how questions can create possibilities for significant learnings and breakthrough actions.

Courage and Authenticity

Asking questions is not always easy, especially asking the tough follow-up questions or questions that require deep and intensive soul searching. The action learning coach needs to be courageous and authentic. He needs to be strong and not intimidated by the rank or expertise or character of the person to whom the question is posed. He should trust his doubts to confirm if agreement and/or clarity truly exist.

Ability to Time Interventions

Finding the ideal time to intervene is an art for the action learning coach. If he intervenes too early, the group or individual may not have sufficient data to adequately respond, and thus there may be a missed opportunity for understanding. If the intervention is too late, there may also be a missed opportunity for learning as well as frustration on the part of the participants because the group has been struggling too long. Experience will help the coach grow more comfortable and confident in timing interventions. And, although timing is important, any time that one intervenes can be an occasion of great learning.

Confidence and Trust in the Process and the People

It is important for the coach to have confidence in her role and to demonstrate this confidence by her relaxed belief in the action learning process and her belief that the group will be successful. She should have confidence that the process will work because it is built on theories and principles (the six components and two rules) that are already in place. The coach should believe that everyone in the group has the necessary abilities to solve the problem; her job is merely to bring out and capitalize on these strengths. The coach's job is to get the group from today to tomorrow (unlike the therapist, who seeks to get the individual from yesterday to today). With a strong confidence in the success of the process and the people, the action learning coach is able to tolerate ambiguity.

Values and Characteristics

The action learning coach, because of the power given him, should be cognizant of how his values as well as his actions affect the group and the action learning process. His presence alone has a significant effect on the group; the members know that the coach may raise questions at any point that will challenge their thinking and actions, decisions made and not made. Therefore, a number of characteristics are fitting for an action learning coach, including openness, patience, honesty and integrity, humility, the ability to be nonjudgmental, and the ability to be reflective. The coach is so subtle and natural in his effectiveness and transformative actions that the group may not realize how powerful and beneficial he is.

Ability to Coordinate and Plan

As noted earlier in this chapter, the action learning coach has a variety of other roles in addition to serving as a group's coach. These other roles require strong coordination skills and the ability to see the big picture and not become lost in details. Since the coach needs to be able to maintain working and supportive relationships with so many people inside and outside the group and even the organization, he must be able to manage many activities at the same time.

Ability to Listen

Successful coaches possess strong listening skills. They should be able to hear what is not said as well as what is said. Careful observation and good note taking allows them to be in tune with who is saying what, how, when, and to whom. Active listening requires a great deal of attention. Strong listening skills enable coaches to acquire a "helicopter" perspective, a holistic view. They must be able to stand apart from the problem and focus on the development of the group.

Strong Commitment to Learning

Action learning coaches are eager to see people learn. As tempting as it may be to become involved in problem solving during a session, the coach continues to focus on the learning, not on the issue or problem being discussed. She understands and appreciates how adults learn and sees learning as a way of life. And she recognizes that learners can only learn for themselves (Boud, Keogh, and Walker, 1985).

Positive Attitude Toward Group Members

The action learning coach respects each person and has a concern for the well-being of all members. He wants them to succeed with the project and to learn from so doing. His ability to empathize and be supportive is very important. He should see members as curious and thoughtful about the problem and about each other. These attitudes generate trust toward him as well as openness among the group members.

Self-Awareness and Self-Confidence

The action learning coach needs to be cognizant of her strengths and limitations. Her self-confidence enables her to be authentic and resilient. Her humility demonstrates that she is willing and able to learn. She should want to be seen as someone who can be trusted, who can handle rivalries, distrust, and anger.

Impact of the Action Learning Coach

The efforts of the action learning coach ultimately build the competence of the group and lead to long-term performance excellence. As

---

Action Coaching at DuPont

Paula Topolosky, DuPont Global Services Business

DuPont's coaches should have the following attributes:

▲ Familiar with group processes
▲ Able not to take control of the group's work
▲ Comfortable being an invisible observer
▲ Helps team learn from its mistakes
▲ Knows how to create a learning environment
▲ Creates energy for learning and growth

---

the group learns and matures, the members become better able to self-correct and are to learn on a continuous basis. The group soon has a strong capacity for learning and changing. The learning coach is a catalyst whose strategic and timely interventions lead to momentous and powerful business results and learning successes.

Checklist for Action Learning Coach

▲ Has the coach been able to guide us in reflecting?
▲ Has a learning and action climate been established?
▲ Are the interventions timely and appropriate?
▲ Does the coach model good questioning and listening skills?
▲ Does she demonstrate confidence in the action learning process?
▲ What is her attitude toward group members?
▲ Does she avoid getting involved with the problem?
▲ What other roles does the action learning coach need to play? Teacher and trainer? Administrator? Promoter? Adviser? Champion?
▲ Is the coach committed to helping us learn and develop?
▲ How could the coach be more effective?

Twelve Steps for Action Learning

Introducing, Implementing, and Sustaining Action Learning

Action learning can be introduced into an organization by any individual or business unit that would like to use this marvelous tool for solving problems and enhancing development. To successfully and systematically introduce, implement, and sustain action learning programs throughout an organization, follow the twelve steps listed in Table 7 and detailed in this chapter. These steps will enable you to optimize the power of action learning and promote its extension throughout the organization. The careful launching of the program will ensure its continuation and will help to overcome the barriers and pitfalls that might derail action learning along the way.

Step 1: Gain Support of Top Management

The first step, and certainly one of the most critical steps in establishing powerful and successful action learning programs in an organization, is to gain the support of top management. The leaders in the organization will become invaluable in launching action learning throughout the organization and assuring the action learning groups that their efforts, strategies, and learnings will be championed and promoted by the organization.

Table 7	*Twelve Steps for Introducing and Implementing Action Learning*

1. Gain support of top management.
2. Conduct a preparatory workshop.
3. Choose projects, problems, or challenges.
4. Select and prepare action learning coach(es).
5. Determine membership and establish the action learning groups.
6. Orient and prepare the action learning group(s).
7. Carry out and implement the action learning sessions.
8. Reframe problems and develop action strategies.
9. Pilot test and recommend actions.
10. Implement action strategies.
11. Finalize activities and capture final learnings of the action learning group.
12. Assess value and power of action learning program and seek ways to expand throughout the organization.

To gain this support, the leaders themselves must first be convinced that action learning will successfully and quickly solve the complex and urgent problems of the organization. They must be willing to acknowledge that some of their existing challenges and problems have been intractable and not well resolved by the existing approaches, such as task groups, training, and outside consultants. These leaders should therefore be open to trying a new approach that will generate quantum improvements for their business and prepare their workers for the challenging and competitive environment surrounding them.

It is very important that top management has a solid understanding of action learning processes and principles. Otherwise, they may not select the appropriate problems, people, or resources for action learning. Or they may withdraw support at the first sign of difficulty or resistance. It is valuable to highlight the fact that action learning enables the organization to have more time in the long term by resolving present problems that are obstructing success in the short term.

If top management becomes convinced that action learning will develop and improve the organizational capacity to provide better products, services, and profits, they will be willing to assign their most critical and urgent problems to the action learning groups and to commit themselves to implementing the solutions and strategies developed by the group. Ideally, they will allow, encourage, and enable the group itself to carry out the solutions it has identified.

Checklist for Top Management Support

▲ Is top management committed to action learning?
▲ Do managers understand the benefits and expectations?
▲ What information or endorsements would enhance their support?
▲ Will they support the action learning groups with time and resources?
▲ Are they aware of and supportive of cultural changes created by action learning?
▲ Is there agreement on overall objectives for the program?
▲ Do they want leadership development as part of the action learning programs? Team building? Organizational culture change?
▲ Are there champions for the action learning sets?
▲ Have the program and its objectives been discussed with potential participants and their managers?
▲ Do managers and participants understand the time factor involved?
▲ How will the recommendations and actions of the action learning groups be handled?

Top management should be aware of the fact that if proposed solutions from the group are rejected or ignored, the energy and efforts of members will quickly dissipate, and much of the power and potential growth of action learning will be impaired. Managers must also understand that if the action learning process is to build leaders and teams, they must allow time and provide appropriate resources (e.g., an action learning coach). Time for learning and development needs to be an integral part of the company's action learning programs. An important question, even at this early stage, is whether the organization will be using internal or external action learning coaches.

A tremendous boost to action learning is to have top management commit to assigning senior managers to action learning groups or to become members of groups themselves. They can also reinforce action learning by allowing groups to use company time to work on organizational problems. Such actions clearly demonstrate their commitment to the program. It is important that leaders maintain management support even when some projects do not achieve immediate success.

What is the best way to secure the support of top management for instituting action learning, and who should introduce action learning to top management? Usually, one or more staff members have heard about or experienced action learning at a conference or in another organization and decide to approach management on their own. These people may emerge as internal action learning champions who offer to submit their own problems and staff to the initial action learning programs. Or they may decide to use action learning at their staff meetings so that they can then show top management how it has been working for them.

Some action learning proponents have found that a more effective approach is to bring an external source—either a leader from another company who is a strong proponent or an experienced action learning coach—into the organization to introduce the principles and benefits of action learning. Often leaders are uncomfortable trying a new system or tool unless they know that other companies have had success with it. Thus, it is valuable to provide examples of companies who have used action learning with wonderful results.

Step 2: Conduct a Preparatory Workshop

Once top management has given its support to introducing action learning into the organization, it is important to get the rest of the organization aboard. The best way to accomplish this goal is to conduct a two-hour action learning workshop that orients everyone to the principles and benefits of action learning. This workshop can also be an opportunity to demonstrate that top management supports the use of action learning in the organization. The workshop should generate enthusiasm from staff members for action learning, encourage them to participate in the program, and in some cases, encourage them to establish action learning groups in their own business units. Therefore, it is critical that the workshop is well delivered, exciting, informative, and thorough so as to build momentum and commitment throughout the organization for action learning.

Arranging the Workshop

A number of key decisions must be made in preparing for the introductory workshop. First, who should conduct the workshop? Is there an internal person who has sufficient knowledge and experience to lead and facilitate the session? Or is it preferable to seek an outside action learning expert or contact an organization such as the Global Institute for Action Learning (www.mgmtconcepts.com/gial/gial.asp)?

To determine the initial interests and concerns of the organization, you may wish to do an informal survey of some of the staff to ascertain the expectations, biases, previous experiences, and misconceptions they may have about action learning. This will allow the planner(s) and presenter to develop the most responsive content and to identify the cases and issues for the workshop that best demonstrate the concerns as well as the benefits of action learning.

Logistics are also important. Provide a convenient and quiet place with sufficient space for the action learning workshop. Arrange for adequate time (ideally two to three hours), not so late or early that people are arriving late or leaving before the workshop has been completed.

You may wish to identify a possible problem or task beforehand that is of interest to most of the attendees and can best demonstrate action learning in a short period of time. If this is not possible, you will need to choose a problem that is offered during the workshop itself. This is sometimes risky, as often no one wishes to volunteer a problem, or the one posed is either too complex to be handled in the abbreviated time period or is unimportant to many of the people attending the workshop.

Ideally, everyone in the organization should have the opportunity to attend the workshop. If there is limited space and only a limited number of people can attend, be sure to recruit the decision makers and those who can quickly put the program into action. It is important to market the workshop extensively to get people to willingly attend. Capture their curiosity. Highlight the benefits. And even if management is requiring everyone to attend, it is still valuable to develop the pre-workshop enthusiasm via word of mouth and/or flyers and in-company media.

Before conducting the workshop, it is beneficial to have top management, or at least some managers, identify problems or tasks around which to build action learning groups. This will harness the momentum created by the workshop, and the energy can be quickly put to use. Other possible pre-workshop issues include whether to seek volunteers or appoint action learning group members, determining time frames for action learning groups, and selecting the action learning coaches.

Content of Workshop

The two-hour workshop has three distinct segments: overview of action learning, demonstration of action learning, and questions and next steps.

Overview of Action Learning (30–45 minutes)

During the first segment of the introductory workshop, the attendees should receive a clear picture about the following topics.

▲ What action learning is and what it is not (i.e., how it is different from quality circles, task forces, outdoor adventures, other problem-solving groups)
▲ The benefits of action learning, namely, the solving of complex and urgent problems and the development of leaders, teams, and organizations
▲ The six components of action learning and two ground rules
▲ The single-problem and multiple-problem types of action learning
▲ Basic principles and procedures of action learning

Demonstration of Action Learning (30–45 minutes)

Action learning should always be demonstrated; nothing explains how and why action learning works or confirms its power and benefits as well as seeing and experiencing the real thing. If the organization has already identified the problem, then the problem is announced and four or five volunteers are requested. If no problem has been identified, the presenter indicates a need for four or five volunteers, one of whom would be willing to share a problem or challenge for the group to work on.

The volunteers should assemble on a stage or in a center space so that the entire audience can observe and hear the interactions of the volunteers as well as the questions and comments of the action learning coach. The volunteers may need to be reminded to speak loudly, even though they are talking to someone a few feet away, so the audience can hear their words.

The presenter/consultant should serve as the action learning coach, as only someone who is experienced and skilled in this role can adequately demonstrate it. The success of the demonstration will depend to a large extent on the competencies of the action learning coach.

The coach indicates, in the interest of time, that he will be telescoping the stages of action learning and jumping more quickly to subsequent stages so as to go through all the stages in the allotted time frame. He also indicates that he will be serving both as the action learning coach and as a teacher who will be highlighting action learning principles and describing events to the audience as they occur. Thus, he will be more active and vocal than he normally would be in the role of action learning coach.

To maintain the interest and learning of the audience, the coach asks the observers to write down questions they would have asked if they were in the action learning group as well as how they would have responded to the questions that the coach is asking. Audience members should not be allowed to ask their questions during the demonstration, as that would destroy the cohesiveness and direction of the group, as well as consume much more time than can be allocated to the demonstration.

During the demonstration, the group should quickly go through the stages of reframing the problem, framing the goal, and developing strategic actions, with perhaps one or two interventions by the coach. After the group has worked for fifteen to twenty-five minutes, the coach should advise the group that it has another five minutes to work on the problem and strategies before he concludes the demonstration with some reflective questions for them. During the course of the demonstration, there will be a number of strategies that the problem presenter or organizational representative will be asked to consider.

When the group has completed its work, the coach asks the problem presenter what action he is going to take based on the ideas and strategies that have arisen. After he has identified his proposed actions, the problem presenter is asked if he has been helped and, if so, how. Inevitably, he has been helped, since he has had the problem clarified and reframed, a result that always occurs when a problem is talked out and explored from a variety of perspectives.

The coach uses the final five to ten minutes to ask the action learning group a number of the postsession questions (see Chapter 7), concurrently alerting the audience as to why he asked the questions that he asked, how and why the follow-up questions were asked, and the impact of the questions and responses.

Questions and Next Steps (15–30 minutes)

The organization's presenter and/or the action learning coach should then ask the audience what questions they have about what they have observed, why the learning coach asked the questions he did, and any principles and practices of action learning that were unclear. It is important that this discussion period focus on the process of what happened, not the content of the problem, since the problem could have been resolved in a number of ways, and members of the audience, because of their different perspectives, might have considered other alternatives. To debate what someone might consider a better alternative would be nonproductive and inconclusive and would miss the point of the demonstration, namely, how and why action learning works.

Another option at this point would be to form a panel at the front of the room composed of a senior leader of the organization, the action learning coach, and the champion of action learning in this company.

Checklist for Assessing Preparatory Workshop

▲ Is top management in support of and present at the workshop?
▲ Are the facilities adequate for presenting and demonstrating action learning?
▲ Is there sufficient time available?
▲ Are all the appropriate people attending?
▲ Are the basic elements of action learning being well covered?
▲ Is the demonstration well organized and set up? Has the organization identified an appropriate problem or challenge for the demonstration?
▲ What is the level of organizational/employee enthusiasm for action learning?
▲ Has a training workshop been developed and conducted that assures that the participants will have (a) a solid understanding of the basic concepts and mechanics of action learning and (b) an appreciation of the value of reflective questioning and continuous learning?
▲ Are outside resources and linkages needed?
▲ Has a time frame been established for setting up the action learning sets? (This is optional, but it is important for participants to have a sense of the level of commitment to action learning by the organization.)

Following questions and discussion about action learning in general, the panel may begin ascertaining the audience's understanding and commitment to action learning, as well as specific actions and steps that the organization will take to establish an action learning program.

Benefits of Preparatory Workshop

The introductory workshop can serve many purposes. Not only does it enable the organization and potential group members to understand action learning, how it works, and how it benefits individuals and the organization, but also it can begin the screening process to determine which managers now believe sufficiently in the tool to initiate an action learning set in their department. It may also identify individuals who would like to join an action learning group. The impetus created by this workshop must quickly be converted into one or many learning groups.

Step 3: Choose Projects, Problems, or Challenges

Choosing the projects or problems that learning groups will work on is at the heart of the action learning process and will have a significant impact on the image and impetus of action learning within the organization. Urgent, complex problems and projects in need of innovative solutions will demonstrate the organization's commitment to action learning and drive the quality of the action as well the quality of the learning. Thus, whether chosen by the individual, by the business unit, or by the organization, the problem should be important, worth resolving, and have a definitive time frame for taking action.

A number of important decisions relative to the choice of the action learning problem need to be made at this juncture.

Single- or Multiple-Problem Sets, or Both?

Action learning can be implemented in either a single-problem or multiple-problem format. Some organizations chose both formats, although the more common approach is a single-problem format. The company should examine the elements, processes, and benefits of each format (see Chapter 1) and choose whichever provides the most value to the organization.

If the single-problem format is selected, only one group should work on that problem. Having more than a single group working on the same problem will dissipate the energy and commitment of the groups as well as diminish the quality of results, even though more total energy may be devoted to the problem. It is much better to have one excellent set of recommendations than to have two mediocre ones, which will occur if two groups tackle the same issue, because the degree of urgency, accountability, and confidence will be lost.

If the organization uses the multiple-problem format, it is important to remember that each person has a limited amount of time for the group to focus on her problem. Thus, the problems that are chosen may need to be less complex than those in a single-problem set (and usually the problems that individuals face are less complicated than those of an organization or department).

What Types of Problems Should Be Chosen?

Any problem that is important to the organization and requires break-through strategies to solve can be considered. Problems may be connected to operations, strategic planning, personnel, management, marketing, or customer relations. They may be significant and complex problems that require several months to complete or quick, urgent, and minor problems that need to be resolved before the end of the day. Examples of potential action learning problems include the following.

▲ Create a new performance appraisal system (Cathay Pacific used action learning to resolve this problem)
▲ Develop a global strategy for the manufacturing division of the company (General Electric)
▲ Handle a disgruntled employee
▲ Build a global solution brand business
▲ Improve information systems
▲ Cut operational costs by $1 billion (Caterpillar)

Whatever problem is chosen, it must be one for which the group has been given the power to develop and implement strategies.

Who Should Choose the Problems?

The problems can be chosen individually or collectively by the members of the action learning group or, as is more common in organization-sponsored action learning programs, by senior management or business unit leaders. The higher the level at which the problems are chosen, the more importance the project will be perceived as having.

Choosing Action Learning Projects at Boeing

In the Global Leadership Program at Boeing, the problems were initially chosen by HR staff. However, as the Boeing Executive Council recognized the high quality of strategic actions developed by the action learning groups, the council decided that it would choose future projects. ■

Who Will Present the Problem/Project at the Initial Session?

The problem presenter is usually the person who is the true owner of the problem. If the problem being considered is an organizational one or one from a business unit, and two or more members of the group are familiar with the problem, then either or all of them can collaborate in presenting the problem and answering questions about the problem.

There may be instances, however, when the problem owner is a manager who is unable to commit herself to attend every meeting of the group (as noted in Chapter 3, attendance at every session is essential for successful problem solving and learning), or she feels her presence would lessen the spontaneity and courage of the group in seeking fresh answers or examining root causes. In these circumstances, she may designate a representative to present the problem and to ensure that the group's proposed strategies will be implemented.

Of course, for the problem owner(s) to be part of the action learning group indicates a strong interest in solving the problem and a stronger commitment to implementing the solutions proposed. If the problem owner is not able to be a full-time member of the group, he should try to be available at the first session to answer questions from the group. He should also be available between sessions to answer questions and to indicate his support or uncertainty relative to strategies being considered (particularly since the problem owner may be the "who knows, who can, and/or who cares" person).

What Aspects of the Problem Should Be Presented?

There is a fine balance between providing too little information about the problem (leaving the members wandering aimlessly) and too much information (thus limiting the range of options that the group considers). To frame his presentation, the problem presenter should take into account the following areas:

▲ What is the background of the project?
▲ How will the organization measure the success of the project team?
▲ What is the critical information you can provide to the team relative to
  ● Business/strategic plans?
  ● Marketing plans?
  ● Competitive information?
  ● Financial results and plans?
  ● Benchmarking data?
▲ Who are the key people within the business/function that the team should meet with? Who will be responsible for scheduling people to meet with the project team (e.g., marketing, financial, manufacturing, legal, sourcing)?
▲ How can you help the project team have access to key stakeholders? Who will schedule these meetings?

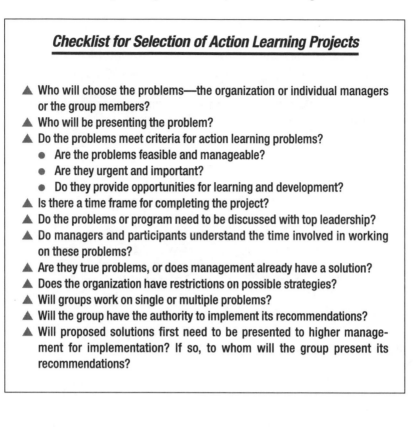

Checklist for Selection of Action Learning Projects

▲ Who will choose the problems—the organization or individual managers or the group members?

▲ Who will be presenting the problem?

▲ Do the problems meet criteria for action learning problems?
  ● Are the problems feasible and manageable?
  ● Are they urgent and important?
  ● Do they provide opportunities for learning and development?

▲ Is there a time frame for completing the project?

▲ Do the problems or program need to be discussed with top leadership?

▲ Do managers and participants understand the time involved in working on these problems?

▲ Are they true problems, or does management already have a solution?

▲ Does the organization have restrictions on possible strategies?

▲ Will groups work on single or multiple problems?

▲ Will the group have the authority to implement its recommendations?

▲ Will proposed solutions first need to be presented to higher management for implementation? If so, to whom will the group present its recommendations?

▲ What key people outside the company should the team engage—customers, suppliers, competitors, trade associations, government agencies?

How Quickly Must the Problem Be Resolved?

Problems usually come with deadlines by which decisions need to be made and tasks need to be completed. If a problem needs to be solved this afternoon, the action learning group will be able to meet only one time. If the decision is due next week, the organization may arrange for the group to meet either on a part-time or full-time basis. If the final action date is a month or six months from now, then the group will probably meet on a part-time basis.

What Authority Should the Problem Presenter Retain?

Many managers are unable or unwilling to delegate power and decision making to a group that might come up with actions with which they are not fully comfortable. It is very difficult to sustain action learning programs if the teams soon recognize that they are merely offering suggestions that may or may not be implemented by the organization. Possible ways of overcoming this resistance include the following.

▲ Relate case studies from organizations such as GE or Boeing that have successfully used action learning over a number of years.

▲ Select a problem that is important but has primarily internal impact and for which there is sufficient time for interim testing and actions.

Step 4: Select and Prepare Action Learning Coach(es)

The overall success of the action learning program is dependent on the quality of coaching, particularly at the initial stages. If coaches perform their roles competently, the program will likely achieve the goals of innovative problem solving and individual, team, and organizational learning. The organization needs to make the following three key decisions relative to action learning coaches.

Should Coaches Be from Within or Outside the Organization?

The organization needs to decide whether it has the resources and trust required to bring in outside coaches (for example, there may be some problems/projects for which the organization would not want outsiders, even coaches, to be present). If the organization chooses to have internal coaches, it will need to determine who will select the coaches and what the selection criteria will be. Additional questions such as "How many coaches should we have available?" and "Should we choose only from our HRD staff or from among our managers or other staff?" must be addressed.

Whether the coaches are internal or external, it is critical that they have a solid understanding of the role, responsibilities, and attributes of the action learning coach. They should be comfortable in asking reflective questions and have confidence and trust in the power of questions rather than their own power. It is important that they have the ability to not involve themselves in the problem, a challenge especially for internal coaches, who, because of their familiarity with the problem or their desire to get a solution that they find favorable or desirable, are tempted to jump into working on the problem rather than focusing on the learning.

Should Coaching Be Rotated Among Members of the Group?

The action learning coach may serve in that role permanently for a particular group, or the role may be rotated during the life of the group (i.e., a different person in that role at each session). The benefit of rotating the coaching role is that it develops some key leadership skills that naturally and effectively occur within that role. For example, when a person serves as a coach, she often will see things that are missed by those involved in the details of the problem solving. Rotating coaches within the group also lessens the time and cost of bringing in outside people. On the other hand, the advantage of an outside person is that the entire group can devote all its attention to the problem.

If an external professional coach is employed, she will need to become familiar with the organization—its culture, mission, structure, and so on. If internal people are chosen, whether on a rotating or permanent basis, it is important that they be properly trained.

Whether internal or external, rotating or permanent, coaches must be qualified and prepared to serve in that role. In Chapter 7, we examined the qualities and competencies needed to successfully coach an action learning group.

If Internal People Serve As Coaches, How Can We Train Them?

Preparing someone to be a coach usually involves having him go through the following three stages.

Participate in an Action Learning Group

Before serving as a coach, one should experience being a member of an action learning group to feel how it is to be asked reflective questions from a coach as well as to participate in the action learning stages and the learning process.

Shadow an Experienced Action Learning Coach

The next stage would be to shadow and observe a learning coach in action. After a session has ended, the coach will ask the observer-coach what happened and the impact of the questions of the coach. The coach will also ask the candidate what he learned from watching the session as an outsider.

Co-Coach

The third stage would be for the person to co-coach an action learning session. The two coaches would agree beforehand on who would intervene during and after the session. At the conclusion of the session, the "senior" coach would ask the aspiring coach how she felt she did, what she did well, what she could do better, and what she learned. The

---

Checklist for Selection and Preparation of Action Learning Coaches

▲ Will we use internal or external action learning coaches?

▲ If using internal staff, how will we train them?

▲ Will members of an action learning group rotate as coaches, or will a person be appointed to serve as the full-time coach?

▲ What attributes and criteria are we seeking for coaches?

▲ Are the learning coaches knowledgeable? Experienced? Comfortable with and trusting of the manner in which the action learning coach facilitates?

---

senior coach would then turn to the other members of the group and ask them what the co-coach did well, what she could have done better, what made her effective, and what questions were the most effective.

Selection and Training of Coaches at Boeing

At various points in the Boeing Global Leadership Program, action learning coaches work with the teams to help members reflect on how they could improve their capabilities as a team and how they could transfer their learnings to other aspects of Boeing operations. The action learning coaches receive an intensive two-day training course prior to serving in that role. In addition, the coaches receive coaching guidance during the initial facilitations of the Boeing teams. Both HRD staff and Boeing managers with no previous group facilitation background have served as action learning coaches. ■

Step 5: Determine Membership and Establish the Action Learning Groups

After the organization has been oriented to action learning and selected the problem(s) for the group(s) to resolve, then decisions need to be made relative to the membership of the action learning groups. The following issues should be resolved at this point.

Who Will Determine Membership in the Groups?

Membership in groups may be by self-selection or members may be determined by the organization, in which case the decision may be made by the sponsor, champion, and/or top leadership.

What Will Be the Number of Members in Each Group?

Action learning is most potent and efficient when the group size is five to six members. If at all possible, membership should not exceed eight members or be less than four. (See Chapter 3 for discussion of group size.)

What Will Be the Criteria for Membership?

The selection of participants should be vigorous to allow for a match between individuals' experiences and project needs. In addition, the organization should seek diversity of perspectives, with people from different business units, different age groups, different disciplines, and so on. Diversity of team members is essential for fresh questions and to capture a wide variety of perspectives.

The organization may feel that it takes too much valuable time to help an outsider "catch up" with people already familiar with the problem. This resistance can best be met by providing successful real cases in which outsiders have helped organizations/groups solve their most difficult problems (e.g., the "pizza man" solution).

Membership should be a combination of those who are familiar with the problem and/or context and those who are not. If all are familiar with the problem or context, the group may have difficulty seeing "beyond the box" and being aware of their assumptions regarding the situation and the solutions. They will tend to say "no" or "we have already tried" too quickly and too often. Those unfamiliar with the context or problem will need more time to get up to speed, and may ask some dumb questions that slow down the initial problem reframing, but this time will be well spent as these people will be able to provide fresh perspectives and insights not possible with internal people only. The unfamiliar members also have the opportunity of achieving the greatest learnings.

Will Members Be Appointed, or Can People Volunteer?

In general, members of single-problem/organization-supported action learning groups are appointed, whereas multiple-problem action learning groups are usually composed of people who have voluntarily chosen to join. The organization may choose to appoint people to be members of specific action learning groups for a number of reasons.

▲ The organization wishes to mix people from different business units for building corporate culture.
▲ The organization is eager to have certain individuals become familiar with particular settings or issues (many executive development programs are like this).
▲ Certain individuals are being considered for potential future leadership positions, and this is an opportunity to assess their true potential.
▲ Top management recognizes the importance of fresh perspectives or diversity and appoints people from different parts of the organization with different backgrounds and experiences.
▲ As a matter of convenience and cost, the organization takes advantage of the availability of certain people.

On the other hand, if employees have the option of volunteering to join action learning groups, their choice may be determined by the following factors.

▲ They care about the problem and/or people in group.
▲ They have knowledge of and interest in the issue.
▲ This problem may have relevance to their work/problems.

Will Groups Include Members from Outside the Organization?

There are significant benefits to including people from outside the organization (e.g., customers, individuals from noncompeting companies, dealers, or suppliers). However, time and costs of using external members must be considered. Of course, the organization must weigh the advantages of gaining fresh ideas and different perspectives versus the potential loss of confidential internal information. Outside perspectives, however, can be helpful in developing and launching new programs. Novartis, for example, formed action learning groups with several noncompeting companies to solve problems submitted by the various companies (see case study in Chapter 2).

Step 6: Orient and Prepare the Action Learning Group(s)

Before beginning the first session, all members of the group must understand the overall principles, the six components, and the two

Checklist for Selection of Members for Action Learning Groups

▲ Will membership be by choice or appointment?
▲ What will be the size of the action learning group?
▲ Will we include members from outside the organization?
▲ Will the groups operate full time or part time?
▲ How often will the groups meet?
▲ Are the most appropriate people in the group?

ground rules that serve as the foundation of action learning practice. Otherwise, the uninformed members will not understand why they are to focus on asking and listening to questions, or why the action learning coach does what he does and with what authority. Members who are not properly oriented may soon become frustrated. They may feel the group is spending too much time clarifying the problem and not getting quickly enough to the solutions.

Also, never assume that group members understand and/or remember the principles and rules of action learning. Even if everyone attended the preparatory workshop (step 2), they may remember it differently or have forgotten some key elements. Therefore, someone in the group, usually the action learning coach, should take a few minutes at the beginning of the first session to clarify the elements of action learning and determine if there are any questions or confusion.

At the first session, a number of logistical and clarifying tasks should be handled before the group begins working on the problem. These tasks include the following.

Arrange and/or Confirm Meeting Dates, Times, Frequency, and Locations

It is important that members attend each meeting of the group. If a member has a conflict that has arisen since the dates were established prior to the group's first meeting, the remaining members of the group should examine how they can help that person rearrange his schedule or priorities, or rearrange the schedule so that meetings are not held when someone cannot attend. It is better to have the group meet less frequently with everyone in attendance than to hold meetings with someone missing. Remember, action learning groups are unique in their "teamness" and in the potency amassed from that teamness; therefore, that quality of time is far more important than the quantity of time spent by the group.

The group needs to confirm once again whether it will be meeting on a full-time, part-time, or one-time basis, a decision that may have been made by top management before the group has its first meeting. Meeting full time may be necessary when the organization must quickly make a decision or immediately develop strategies for an issue or crisis. The benefit of full-time action learning groups is that the members are less likely to be interrupted by other job responsibilities. It is important, however, that the members not be pulled out of the group and that they concentrate their energies and efforts on solving the problem and developing strategies.

Many problems allow for the action learning group to meet on a part-time basis over a longer period of time. Meeting part time has many advantages. It allows for members to carry out their regular, on-the-job responsibilities; thus, the organization does not need to deploy other resources to cover their absence. (Although it is certainly possible for action learning sessions to occur outside working hours, this would indicate that the organization is not very committed to action learning.) Meeting part time also gives members the time and opportunity to gather information and/or apply strategies between sessions. In addition, individuals and the organization itself can more easily see growth and development as leaders, team members, and professionals.

Part-Time Projects at Bristol-Myers Squibb

Bristol-Myers Squibb, a global leader in personal and health care, has used part-time action learning projects for nearly ten years to resolve its most complex challenges. Action learning projects have included development of marketing strategies, examination of plant closures, and means to increase customer support. ■

More and more organizations are creating full-time action learning programs, especially as part of their leadership development efforts. Companies such as Boeing, Unilever, DuPont, and Baxter place high-potential leaders in one- to three-month action learning projects to work on major company challenges as well as to develop key leadership competencies. Some organizations, such as GE, establish one- to two-day weekday or weekend action learning programs. Others prefer projects to last for one to two months. Of course, the scheduling of sessions is determined by both the problems of the organization and the developmental needs of the group members.

Some action learning groups meet for one time only, as the problem has an urgent time frame and the issue is clearly defined. The availability of preferred group members (distance, other commitments) make the time and resource availability a now-or-never proposition.

Organizations should be careful not to overly restrict the time available for the group to work on the problem. Too short a time period may result in a less than stellar understanding of—and therefore poor solutions to—the problem. Gaining a systems perspective and identifying the points of greatest leverage require time during and between sessions.

Specific Learning Purposes of the Action Learning Sessions

Organizations and the group members can identify both the specific individual and organizational learning purposes for the group. Most groups have a goal to develop the individuals' competencies, whether leadership competencies that are expected of all leaders in this organization (e.g., as at Boeing) or the specific competencies identified for this individual (e.g., as in the U.S. Department of Agriculture). Individual members may ask the rest of the group to help them develop some specific personal skills such as handling conflict, being a better listener, or tolerating ambiguity. Organizations may also seek goals that change the culture and competencies of the organization or develop team building and membership skills. The organization may also be expecting the learnings to be systematically transferred throughout the organization, and thus, time and effort to accomplish those goals need to be arranged by the action learning coach.

The organization's and individual's developmental goals are determined either before the first session or when the coach completes the reflective learning at the end of the first session. The value of introducing the specific developmental goals up front is that everyone will be consciously or subconsciously thinking about them and therefore better able to provide specifics when the coach asks for examples of leadership behavior or opportunities for application.

Role and Style of the Coach

Although the role and responsibilities of the coach may be understood by the group, it is wise to remind people how you will be working as a coach. For example, the coach may sit a couple feet back from the table and lean forward when preparing for an intervention. Or, she might like the group to focus on the learning and to continue responding to her questions until she gives a signal to continue the problem solving.

Scheduling of the First Session

The coach will confirm the timing of the different stages of the session. For example, if it is a multiple-problem set, he will allocate an approximate amount of time for each person, so that there is reflection/learning time after each session and a more comprehensive learning time at the end of the program. Table 8 shows a sample schedule for a multiple-problem group with five members. In a single-problem session, the coach may advise the group when they have approximately thirty minutes left to work on the problem, since he is reserving the last fifteen minutes for final reflections and learnings. If the coach does not provide a time warning, members may be surprised and even upset that they had to stop working on the problem. They may push for a little more time, the result of which is that there is little or no time left for the final learnings, which is when the most significant developments generally occur. The power and value of the coach will be diminished, and the group may continue to erode his time and power as they may feel that it is not as important as solving the problem.

Acknowledging the Sponsor of the Group

The sponsor is the business unit or person who has selected this problem and has made a commitment to implement the solutions proposed by the group, whether they are carried out by the group members themselves or by other people identified by the sponsor. In an organization-sponsored action learning group, it is important to confirm the identity of the sponsor of the problem. Knowing who the sponsor is could be relevant as the group develops specific strategies. Often the sponsor is a key person who may have the knowledge, power, and/or passion needed to implement the strategies.

If the problem sponsor is not able to be a member of the group, she may appoint someone else to serve as a member of the group. If neither the sponsor nor her representative can be a group member, then it is important that one or the other is available at the first meeting to provide the initial description of the problem and to answer questions from the group. This will help the group reframe the problem as well as assist members in identifying and clarifying the business issue and deliverables.

Table 8	*Sample Schedule for Multiple-Problem Session, Five Members*
9:00	Welcome and planning of session
9:10	Presenter 1 (20–30 minutes)
9:35	Action learning coach, capturing of learnings (5–10 minutes)
9:40	Presenter 2 and learnings
10:10	Presenter 3 and learnings
10:40	Break
10:50	Presenter 4 and learnings
11:20	Presenter 5 and learnings
11:50	Final reflections and learnings
12:00	Adjourn

Identifying the Champion of the Group

Note that the champion and the sponsor may be one and the same person. The champion is the organizational person who ensures that action learning programs are given high visibility and acceptance in the organization. She is someone who understands the nature of the program, thinks it is important, and can be influential in making sure the group gains access to the necessary resources. She will work with key leadership in the organization to be sure that action learning programs are supported and implemented. This person seeks to ensure that appropriate company people cooperate in providing time, answers, and resources to the action learning members, both in the group setting and occasionally in one-to-one situations.

Confidentiality of Action Learning

For action learning to work, all group members must feel confident that their comments about the organization, customers, employees, and each other are kept in the room. Without confidence in the confidentiality of the group, problem presenters and members may not be willing to share the crucial information that they possess and may not be honest and frank in responding to questions. The quality of the problem solving and the group's development, accordingly, will be severely hampered.

The importance of confidentiality can be addressed organization-wide if the company establishes this norm for all its action learning

---

Checklist for Orientation and Preparation of Action Learning Groups

▲ Are the members clearly oriented to the principles of action learning?

▲ Are they aware of how action learning is different from task forces and other problem-solving groups?

▲ Is the role of the action learning coach clear and accepted?

▲ Are there any specific organizational or individual learning goals?

▲ Will we be using single- and/or multiple-problem groups?

▲ Have set members agreed to processes and norms relative to airspace, asking questions, and reflection?

▲ Is there agreement on ground rules relative to confidentiality, starting and stopping on time, being supportive, and taking action between meetings?

▲ Have members agreed on future dates for set meetings and committed to attending them regularly?

▲ Do we have access to the necessary outside resources and knowledge?

▲ Is there a sense of ownership and responsibility for the problem?

▲ Have members identified a place convenient for participants?

▲ Is the group clear as to its sponsor and champion (if any)?

---

programs: any information shared within an action learning session is considered confidential and may be shared outside the group only with the approval of all members.

Step 7: Carry Out and Implement the Action Learning Sessions

Based on decisions made earlier relative to the time frame and deadlines for making decisions and taking action, the group may meet either on a full-time or part-time basis. The frequency of part-time meetings may thus be daily, weekly, or monthly. For example, if external events require an earlier decision point, and the problem is urgent, the group could establish a new schedule.

The length of meetings may range from one to three hours (usually the minimum for multiple-problem groups) to a full day. Of course, the frequency and length of sessions can be adjusted if it is determined that more frequent or longer meetings are necessary.

Action learning groups are more valuable when there is more than one session and a reasonable amount of time between sessions, since the group can go only so far in reframing the problem and developing action plans during the session. Information and support from resources outside the group may be needed before the group can go any further. In addition, the group and/or individual members may need to carry out actions developed by the group, report back to the group at the next session, and only then plan further actions based on the results of earlier actions. Also, individuals need time to ascertain whether their competencies are being developed to have more opportunities for developing these preselected skills.

If, however, there is too long a time between meetings (i.e., more than one month), there may be missed opportunities for developing and implementing the action, particularly if this is, as it should be, an urgent problem. In addition, momentum for working on the problem, as well as the cohesiveness of the group, may be lost. Prior decisions and learnings may be lost as well. Also, group members may return to their previous problem-solving culture of making statements and jumping to conclusions, of debating rather than dialoguing.

Normally, the first session(s) will focus on the stages of problem reframing and goal framing, and later sessions will be spent primarily on the stages of developing strategies and taking actions.

It is important for the coach to assert his responsibility for retaining sufficient time to capture learnings and assist the group in developing its problem-solving abilities. Although group members may have the natural tendency to devote all their time to working on the problem and to depart immediately after the next action steps have been determined, the coach needs to insist on having the entire group take time to examine its growth and to identify areas for improvement. This resistance is usually overcome the first time the group sees improved performance as a result of the time they spent in "mining the learning."

During the sessions, a number of pitfalls and difficulties may emerge. These can include the following.

One Member Dominating the Group

This problem does not normally arise in action learning groups, since an individual should be making statements only in response to a question. New questions are not raised until the previous question has been answered. If a person begins to try to take over the group, the coach can simply ask the group, "What is the quality of our questions at this time?" Everyone, including the person who may be dominating the group, will quickly recognize that the group norm and action learning ground rules are being violated, and the group's balance will immediately be restored.

Conflict

In any problem-solving situation, with individuals with different personalities and different perspectives, and with a problem that has multiple possible solutions, there will inevitably be some disagreements and even hostile feelings expressed. Because of the intensity within the context of action learning, there will be times when emotions run high. However, if they become too high, the resulting stress will cause people to back off, and they may become concerned about offending someone inside or outside the group.

Problem- or strategy-based conflicts are fine as long as they are legitimate and are openly examined. Personality conflicts, on the other hand, are not beneficial for a group. These types of conflict, however, can be overcome, since the coach brings above the table what, in most groups, stays below the table. The coach merely asks, "How are we doing as a group?" One or more individuals will say, "Not well." Asking for examples and why this conflict is occurring will enable the group to recognize how the conflict contributes to and detracts from the effectiveness of the group, how to best deal with the conflict, and how to reinforce earlier agreed-upon norms and/or introduce new norms. Upon resumption of work on the problem, the group will return to high levels of performance.

Members Not Showing Up

Of course, serious emergencies can arise when busy people attempt to fulfill commitments made weeks or months in advance. If the absence is known long in advance, the group may decide to reschedule or skip that session. If it is sudden and unexpected, the group needs to discuss how to update and assist the absent member in "reexperiencing" what the group did at this missed session. If, however, a person has withdrawn from the group for significant professional or personal reasons, the group needs to decide whether there is still time to enroll a new person or to continue with one less person.

Members Not Willing to Share Information

The power of action learning relies on the client/presenter truly trusting and counting on the group to assist him or her. If the presenter holds back information and/or lacks commitment to take action, the members will soon lose their interest and energy to help. One way of overcoming such resistance on the part of the client would be to allow her a "pass"

Checklist for the Implementation of the Action Learning Sessions

▲ Is there sufficient time between meetings to allow for necessary information collection and action?

▲ Has necessary time been reserved at the end of meetings for reflections, learnings, and applications?

▲ Do managers and participants understand the time involved?

▲ Are members interested in and committed to solving problems?

▲ Do members listen to, respect, and learn from others?

▲ Do they attend all meetings?

▲ Has sufficient time been allocated for learning?

▲ Is everyone committed to attending each meeting for the entire meeting?

▲ Is there a balance between problem solving/strategizing and reflection/learning?

▲ Are participants practicing new kinds of behavior, for example, tolerating ambiguity, continually rethinking decisions and looking at probes from a new angle, taking risks, challenging others, searching out rather than receiving information, reflecting?

▲ How are we handling conflict, domination by an individual, member absence, and discomfort in sharing information (if these occur)?

---

at this session. As she sees the successes of fellow colleagues who share information and concerns, she may recognize that she has forfeited a valuable opportunity and will be sure never to do so again.

Step 8: Reframe Problems and Develop Action Strategies

Action learning groups have definitive time periods in which to produce clear results. Each group should take an appropriate and diligent amount of time to reframe the problem and establish the goal(s) that will have the most significant, long-term benefit to the organization or individual. It is important to remember that the group may often end up working on a goal not directly related to the originally presented problem, but one that is clearly the most appropriate goal for resolving the situation faced by the organization or individual in the most effective way.

The group knows it is accountable and responsible for resolving the problem. The reputation and future status of the organization, as well as the success of the organization itself, may depend on the quality of the group's strategies and the success of its actions. Thus, there should be full commitment to solving the problem. It is also important for the group to see each problem as unique, rather than as similar to a past problem and requiring a past solution. The group should avoid the tendency to jump to solutions too quickly or accept an easy, mundane solution.

As we noted in Chapter 5, the action learning group undergoes three phases, or systems, as members examine and work on the problem. These are *System Alpha,* or situation analysis; *System Beta,* the survey, hypothesis, experiment, audit, and review stage; and *System Gamma,* the mental predisposition of members and the organization to the situation. While group members are working on the problem and developing strategies, they need to monitor organizational support and commitment for participants and projects. It is important for the group to have clarity on the boundaries regarding what is open to change and what is not.

The strategies must take into account the overall impact of the various alternatives being considered so that the actions do not create greater problems. This is why action learning groups pilot test possible strategies to study the effects of those strategies and to learn from them. Throughout the problem reframing and strategy developing, the group should be examining and tapping potential sources of power, passion, and knowledge so that the plan, when fully completed, will be implemented, rather than remain a great idea only. Outside company resources and links may need to be identified as well.

Finally, it is important that specific actions to be taken are identified at the end of each action learning session. Clearly identify who will be responsible and by what dates. At the beginning of the next action learning meeting, the status and results of these actions should then be reviewed. Action learning groups take agreed-upon actions between sessions until the final decisions and overall actions have been determined and implemented.

Activities and Recommendations of Learning Groups at Boeing

The Global Leadership Program is divided into three phases: introduction, in-country, and report-out. The introduction consists of three days in a location within the United States and is filled with introductions, orientation, and guest speakers from within and outside of Boeing. The second phase of the program is spent entirely within the country selected by the corporate executive board as a

Checklist for Reframing Problems and Developing Action Strategies

▲ What is the quality of problem framing?

▲ What type of problem is it—technical or adaptive?

▲ Have we identified the real problem versus the presenting problem?

▲ Are our goals specific, measurable, feasible, and beneficial to the organization?

▲ Are we asking fresh questions and taking risks?

▲ Have the obstacles been identified?

▲ What is our level of commitment to solving the problem?

▲ Are we committed to innovative, high-quality solutions and strategies rather than quick solutions?

▲ Have we looked for and linked up with the power, passion, and knowledge?

▲ Have we identified outside resources and links that may be needed?

▲ Are actions plans specific and part of each meeting?

▲ Have the actions to be taken been clearly identified at each meeting, including the responsible person(s) and the specific dates?

▲ Are strategic actions recorded and then reviewed at the next meeting?

▲ Are the best-leveraged solutions chosen?

▲ Have learnings from our actions been achieved?

▲ Have we considered the impact of our strategies?

strategically important country. The three weeks are spent traveling to major portions of the country, interviewing business leaders, hearing from country experts, and being immersed in the culture. After approximately ten days into this phase, the Boeing leaders are introduced to a specific business issue selected by the corporate executive board as an important and current issue for the company. The participants form action learning teams to develop solutions and recommendations to present to Boeing's corporate decision makers. The members of the action learning teams return to the United States for the final two days of the program. These days are spent reviewing, refining, and practicing the team's presentation before the executive committee at a regularly scheduled session. Boeing has incorporated many of the recommendations from Global Leadership participants, adding much to the company's global success. ■

Step 9: Pilot Test and Recommend Actions

Only by testing the group's ideas in practice will members know whether the proposed strategies are effective and practical and whether there are any unanticipated consequences of the actions. Action learning groups should, when possible, pilot test part or all of their strategies. This will enable them to fine-tune the strategy, gain greater confidence in their plans, and acquire support from the organization. It also allows the group to choose between possible strategies so as not to have too many strategies to implement. Finally, reflecting on the pilot testing continues the group's learning and enables them to improve the final plans and actions.

There are three possible options for implementing the strategies and actions devised by the action learning group.

▲ The group may have already been given the power to implement the strategy as part of its original charter when it was formed. The group can therefore immediately apply the strategies and solutions it has developed.
▲ The group may need to take its plan and recommendations to top management for approval. If approved, the group will be expected to implement the strategy.
▲ The group presents its recommendations to top management. Top management then appoints or creates another group or business unit to implement the action strategies.

If the group is not taking, or cannot take, action before having it approved by an outside group (e.g., top management, the sponsor, a business unit director), then it should take the necessary time and effort to carefully craft a strategy for convincing the powers that be to take the recommended actions. This may involve both a rational and emotional presentation of the facts and figures behind the group's decision and recommendations. Some organizations (e.g., Boeing, GE) will want to hear about the group's learnings as well as their strategies.

Step 10: Implement Action Strategies

Taking action is an important element of any action learning group's activities. If the group is merely making recommendations, there will be diminished commitment as well as diminished learning. There is less learning without action, since we cannot be sure if our ideas will work. Also, we do not know if we have learned how to manage unless

---

Checklist for Pilot Testing and Making Recommendations

▲ How can we pilot test the strategies?
▲ What have we learned from the pilot testing?
▲ Does the action learning group have the authority to implement the action strategies?
▲ If not, who are the people who will determine the actions to be taken?
▲ What is important to the decision makers?
▲ How will the group's recommendations be handled and implemented?
▲ What communications between the top management, the sponsors, and the group have occurred during the life of the action learning group?
▲ Will we be sharing our learnings as well as our recommendations?

---

we manage—just as we can only learn how to serve a tennis ball by actually hitting the ball.

Since action learning is not only about developing a recommendation (as with many problem-solving groups), but also about taking action, the preferred option for the organization is to have the group implement its own strategies. There are often situations, however, in which this is not possible, and only another group or business unit has the authority to implement the solution. This might occur because

▲ The proposed solution requires the actions of people throughout the organization and/or around the world
▲ Only top management has the power or connections to implement the strategy
▲ The strategy developed by the action learning group involves people not originally seen as essential by top management and/or the group

If the organization chooses to have someone other than the action learning group implement the solution, it is important that the results gained by the new group's implementation be referred back to the original action learning group so that they have a final opportunity to learn about the quality and impact of their action strategies.

The actions undertaken should be monitored for unanticipated troubles or benefits of the strategy. For each action item, there should be a clear indication of who will be responsible for implementation, what the specific time frame is, and what the anticipated results at

---

Checklist for Implementation of Actions

▲ Who will implement the strategies?

▲ If the action learning group is not implementing the strategies, how will it be informed of the results?

▲ Are the strategies for the actions clear, systems oriented, and time based?

▲ Are there unexpected difficulties in implementation?

▲ Were problems resolved and actions taken?

▲ How effective were the actions taken?

▲ Is there sufficient support from top management?

▲ Is there follow-up to the action learning actions?

---

critical junctures are. Solutions should complement and build upon the other work going on in the organization. The positive changes generated by action learning must be consistent with organizational values and messages. Lastly, it is important to keep decision makers and implementers up-to-date on actions—both the successes and the failures.

Step 11: Finalize Activities and Capture Final Learnings of the Action Learning Group

Action learning groups exist for specific purposes and for a limited time period. When the group has accomplished its action and learning purposes, it is disbanded. Before the group breaks up, however, the action learning coach, organizational champion, and other key organizational figures should conduct a summative assessment of the overall results of the action learning group. They should analyze what worked and what did not and why. The effectiveness of the proposed strategies, the most significant learnings, and the degree to which those learnings were transferred, as well as the present impact of those transferals, should all be scrutinized.

The action learning group, together with top management, should identify how future action learning programs could be more effective in selecting problems and membership, interacting with the organiza-

---

Action Learning Lessons at Oxford University Press

▲ Ensure that you have top management support and that sponsors of projects fully understand their vital role. We insist not only on briefing sponsors, but also on training them alongside their participants before the project work begins. You must have the best people tackling the projects and people who will manage their time effectively to complete the work.

▲ The project content is vital. Pick inappropriate projects and the program is doomed to failure. The projects must be big, but not so big as to overwhelm a project leader and the team working on it for six months.

▲ The brief for the project may need to be renegotiated a number of times. It must also have some finite results. Beware, too, of continuous improvement fatigue. Participants, and the organization generally, can tire of the same messages being circulated. The projects need to be marketed effectively and presented imaginatively.

▲ The purpose of an action learning program is that action take place. Participants should always be encouraged to act and to make decisions, not just recommend courses of action. This is the very essence of the action learning program. (Marsh and Wood, 2001)

---

tion, and implementing recommendations. Finally, there should be an exploration of how other learning and training programs in the organization can better connect with the learning and development inherent in action learning.

Step 12: Assess Value and Power of Action Learning Program and Seek Ways to Expand Throughout the Organization

The power and successes of action learning programs should lead to strong and visible commitment, as well as further participation, from top management. When properly initiated and implemented, action learning provides a unique and powerful tool for simultaneously and effectively accomplishing five benefits for the organization: (1) solving the company's most urgent and important problems, tasks, issues, and/or challenges; (2) transforming the company into a learning orga-

---

Checklist for Final Work and
Learning of the Action Learning Group

▲ Have the learnings been applied throughout the organization?
▲ What is the quality of individual development and learning? Of team development and learning?
▲ Are the greater, long-term benefits and leveraging of learning valued?
▲ Is there commitment to team and individual learnings?
▲ Has there been a review of the learning?
▲ Has there been a systematic analysis of how the learning has been applied to other parts of the organization?
▲ What were the major benefits to the members of the action learning program?
▲ Have verbal or written reports been prepared for clients, managers, and others interested?
▲ How can future action learning programs in the company be improved?
▲ What are the follow-up plans?

---

nization that adapts quickly to the changing environment; (3) developing leaders who can be effective in the twenty-first century; (4) building high-performing and self-directing work teams; and (5) generating enhanced and continuous learning and professional development of all employees. At periodic junctures throughout the action learning program, the organization should carefully examine and assess how the program is succeeding in attaining these benefits.

Assessing the Benefits of Action
Learning at Johnson & Johnson

William Welden, Worldwide Chairman, Pharmaceutical Group

Action learning has significantly enhanced Johnson & Johnson's leadership development and has improved our business by developing new and exciting business opportunities.

Six-Month Follow-up at the U.S. Department of Agriculture

Two action learning groups at the U.S. Department of Agriculture met virtually six months after completing their leadership development program. The participants exchanged success stories on how their leadership skills had continued to build and discussed new leadership areas that they wish to develop. They also identified ways to improve future action learning programs in the department. ■

Problem Solving

As action learning groups achieve successes in resolving the problems and tasks assigned to them, the organization should begin seeing those skills and the "can-do" attitude transferred to the problems that are confronted on a daily basis. The organization should observe greater competencies to systematically resolve the most complex problems. Problems should be easily reframed, goals should become more strategic, and actions taken should result in problems staying solved rather than arising in a mutated form elsewhere in the organization. Finally, the organization should see more team-solved rather than individual-solved problems.

Learning Organization

The most powerful potential benefit of action learning is its ability to transform an organization into a learning organization, since learning organizations, in the words of Walter Wriston, former CEO of Citicorp, "will blow the competition away." Learning organizations have significant competitive advantages because they learn more quickly how to capture knowledge and convert it into products, services, and profits. As mini–learning organizations, action learning groups model and exemplify the essence of what makes learning organizations so powerful.

▲ Learning is performance based and tied to business objectives.
▲ Importance is placed on learning processes (learning how to learn).
▲ Continuous opportunities exist to develop knowledge, skills, and attitudes.
▲ Learning becomes a part of all action and work, a part of everybody's job description.

Leadership

A new kind of leadership is needed in the global, knowledge-driven twenty-first century. Leadership work by Collins (2001), Goleman

(2002), Marquardt and Berger (2000), and Sashkin and Sashkin (2003) points to a need for leaders with transformational abilities, learning skills, emotional intelligence, ethical standards, problem-solving and project management strengths, self-awareness and understanding, and servant-leadership qualities. Action learning programs provide opportunities for all of these competencies to be practiced and developed. Organizations that have implemented action learning should be able to see remarkable differences in how their managers lead and in the successes accruing from these new leadership attributes. Companies using action learning should have greater confidence that the future leadership of their organization will be in good shape.

Teamwork

Teams have become the dominant instrument in organizations as they seek to handle the complexity of organizational life and respond to the growing expectations of customers. Action learning has the ability to generate ideal teams that have extraordinary capacities to solve problems and work in an effective and harmonious manner. Organizations should assess whether their teams—be they business units, task forces, or committees—are now more effective and successful.

Individual Development and Learning

Employees who have experienced action learning should be demonstrating a new capacity to learn as well as develop the skills they need to be successful in their jobs. They should be more confident, innovative, and willing to take risks; have a systems perspective; be able to handle uncertainty and ambiguity; be more comfortable in teams; and be able to assume leadership roles when called upon.

Finally, in its efforts to fully tap the benefits of action learning, the organization should continue to search for additional ways of expanding the use of action learning and thereby expand the organization's ability to solve problems and develop its people.

Optimizing the Power of Action Learning

Action learning has rapidly become one of the most popular and powerful tools used by organizations around the world. Its capacity to provide the tremendous benefits of problem solving and individual, team, and organizational development at minimal costs and in relatively short time frames makes it a cost-effective resource for corporate success. Action learning can truly be a rich treasure for your organization!

Checklist of Impact of Action Learning on Organization

▲ What are the most significant benefits provided by the action learning programs?

▲ Are organizational problems being better resolved?

▲ What other problems or parts of the organization can apply action learning?

▲ Are employees better at framing and solving problems?

▲ Is action learning more effective in solving problems than other mechanisms used in the organization?

▲ Has the organization become a learning organization?

▲ Is the learning culture, as practiced in action learning sets, permeating the organization and how people learn?

▲ Are we placing a high priority on learning in all of our operations and planning, as we do in the action learning sets?

▲ Do we expand our learning via ongoing questioning and reflection?

▲ Is learning that is acquired in one situation applied throughout the organization?

▲ Have we created new resources and networks for improving our learning?

▲ Are we creating more organizationwide opportunities for learning?

▲ Is learning rewarded and measured?

▲ How are we acquiring, storing, transferring, and testing our knowledge?

▲ How has leadership developed?

▲ What is the quality of our teams?

▲ Are people working better together?

▲ Are we better able to work in teams? To manage group processes?

▲ Are we more effective in managing projects?

▲ Are we better at systems thinking? Are we taking more and better risks?

▲ Are we more innovative?

▲ Do we manage uncertainty and ambiguity more effectively?

▲ What were the major benefits to the employees who were members of the action learning program?

▲ How can the organization's future action learning programs be improved?

References

Argyris, C. 1982. *Reasoning, learning, and action*. San Francisco: Jossey-Bass.
Argyris, C. 1991. Teaching smart people how to learn. *Harvard Business Review* 69, no. 3: 99–109.
Argyris, C., and D. Schön. 1978. *Organizational learning: A theory of action perspective*. Reading, Mass.: Addison-Wesley.
Bandler, R., and J. Grinder. 1982. *Reframing: Neuro-linguistic programming and the transformation of meaning*. Salt Lake City, Utah: Real People Press.
Bandura, A. 1977. *Social learning theory*. Englewood Cliffs, N.J.: Prentice-Hall.
Bannan-Ritland, B. 2001. An action learning framework for teaching instructional design. *Performance Improvement Quarterly* 14, no. 2: 37–51.
Barker, A. E. 1998. Profile of action learning's principal pioneer—Reginald W. Revans. *Performance Improvement Quarterly* 11, no. 1: 9–22.
Barth, R. 1981. In the eyes of the led. *Executive* 6, no. 3: 30–33.
Bass, B. 1985. *Leadership and performance beyond expectations*. New York: Free Press.
Battram, A. 1999. *Navigating complexity: The essential guide to complexity theory in business and management*. London: The Industrial Society.
Beaty, L., T. Bourner, and P. Frost. 1993. Action learning: Reflections on becoming a set member. *Management Education & Development* 24, no. 4: 350–367.
Bennett, R. 1990. Effective set advising in action learning. *Journal of European Industrial Training* 14, no. 7: 28–30.
Bierema, L. 1998. Fitting action learning to corporate programs. *Performance Improvement Quarterly* 11, no. 1: 86–107.
Bion, W. 1991. *Experiences in groups*. London: Tavistock.
Block, P. 1999. *Flawless consulting*. San Francisco: Jossey-Bass.
Boddy, D. 1981. Putting action learning into practice. *Journal of European Industrial Training* 5, no. 5: 2–20.
Boud, D., R. Keogh, and D. Walker. 1985. *Reflection: Turning experience into learning*. London: Kogan Page.
Bowerman, J., and J. Peters. 2000. Action learning: The lessons for Workers Compensation Board. *Human Resource Management International Digest* 8, no. 2: 26–28.

Brooks, A. 1998. Educating human resource development leaders at the University of Texas, Austin: The use of action learning to facilitate university/workplace collaboration. *Performance Improvement Quarterly* 11, no. 2: 48–58.

Brown, J. S., and P. Duguid. 1991. Organizational learning and communities of practice: Toward a unified view of working, learning, and innovation. *Organization Science* 2, no. 1: 40–57.

Brown, S., and K. Eisenhardt. 1998. *Competing on the edge: Strategy as structured chaos.* Cambridge: Harvard Business School Press.

Bruner, J. 1974. *Toward a theory of instruction.* Cambridge: Harvard Business School Press.

Bunning, R. L. 1993. Action learning: Developing managers with a bottom-line payback. *Executive Development* 7, no. 4: 3–6.

Butterfield, S., K. Gold, and V. Willis. 1998. Creating a systematic framework for the transfer of learning from an action learning experience. *Academy of HRD Proceedings,* 490–496.

Casey, D. 1997. The role of the set advisor. In M. Pedler, ed., *Action learning in practice,* 3rd ed. Aldershot, England: Gower.

Christie, A., and E. Sandelands. 2000. The knowledge harvest: Ensuring you reap what you sow. *Journal of Workplace Learning* 12, no. 3: 83–88.

Collier, J., and R. Esteban. 1999. Governance in the participation organization: Freedom, creativity, and ethics. *Journal of Business Ethics* 21, nos. 2/3: 173–188.

Collins, J. 2001. *Good to great.* New York: HarperCollins.

Confessore, G. J., and S. J. Confessore. 1992. *Guideposts to self-directed learning.* King of Prussia, Pa. Organization Design and Development, Inc.

Cooperrider, D., P. Sorensen, and T. Yaeger. 2001. *Appreciative inquiry: An emerging direction for organization development.* Champaign, Ill.: Stipes.

Cusins, P. 1995. Action learning revisited. *Industrial and Commercial Training* 27, no. 4: 3–10.

Davenport, T., and L. Prusak. 1998. *Working knowledge: How organizations manage what they know.* Boston: Harvard Business School Press.

Densten, I., and J. Gray. 2001. Leadership development and reflection: What is the connection? *International Journal of Educational Management* 15, no. 3: 119–125.

Dewey, J. 1933. *How we think: Restatement of the relation of reflective thinking to the educative process.* Boston: D.C. Heath.

Dewey, J. 1997 (1916). *Democracy in education.* New York: The Free Press.

Dilt, R. 1999. *Slight of mouth: The magic of conversational belief change.* Capitola, Calif.: Meta Publications.

Dilworth, R. L. 1995. The DNA of the learning organization. In S. Chawla and J. Renesch, eds., *Learning organizations.* Portland, Ore.: Productivity Press.

Dilworth, R. L. 1996. Action learning: Bridging academic and workplace domains. *Employee Counseling Today* 8, no. 6: 48–56.

Dilworth, R. L. 1998. Action learning in a nutshell. *Performance Improvement Quarterly* 11, no. 1: 28–43.

Dilworth, R. L., and V. Willis. 2003. *Action learning: Images and pathways.* Malabar, Fla.: Krieger Publishing.

Dixon, N. M. 1996. *Perspectives on dialogue.* Greensboro, N.C.: Center for Creative Leadership.

Dixon, N. M. 1998a. Action learning: More than just a task force. *Performance Improvement Quarterly* 11, no. 1: 44–58.

Dixon, N. M. 1998b. Building global capacity with global task teams. *Performance Improvement Quarterly* 11, no. 1: 108–112.

Foy, N. 1977. Action learning comes to industry. *Harvard Business Review 55*, no. 5: 158–168.

Freire, P. 1973. *Education for critical consciousness.* New York: Seabury Press.

Froiland, P. 1994. Action learning: Taming real problems in real time. *Training* 31, no. 1: 27–34.

Fulmer, W. 2000. On the edge. *CIO* 13, no. 14: 202–212.

Garratt, R. 1997. The power of action learning. In M. Pedler, ed., *Action learning in practice,* 3rd ed. Aldershot, England: Gower.

Gharajedaghi, J. 1999. *Systems thinking: Managing chaos and complexity.* Boston: Butterworth-Heinemann.

Gibson, M., and P. Hughes. 1987. The supervisory process in action learning. *Management Education and Development* 18, no. 4: 264–276.

Goleman, D. 1996. *Emotional intelligence.* New York: Bantam Books.

Goleman, D. 2000. *Working with emotional intelligence.* New York: Bantam Books.

Gregory, M. I. 1994a. Accrediting work-based learning: Action learning—a model for empowerment. *The Journal of Management Development* 13, no. 4: 41.

Gregory, M. I. 1994b. Accrediting work-based learning: Action learning—a model for empowerment. *Industrial and Commercial Training* 26, no. 4: 41–52.

Hammer, M., and S. Stanton. 1997. The power of reflection. *Fortune* 136, no. 10: 291–294.

Heifetz, R., and D. Laurie. 1997. The work of leadership. *Harvard Business Review 75*, no. 1: 124–134.

Heiman, M., and J. Slomianko. 1990. *Learning to learn on the job.* Alexandria, Va.: ASTD Press.

Henderson, I. 1993. Action learning: A missing link in management development? *Personnel Review* 22, no. 6: 14–24.

Hergenhahn, B. R. 1988. *An introduction to theories of learning,* 3rd ed. Englewood Cliffs, N.J.: Prentice Hall.

Hofstede, G. 1992. *Cultures and organizations.* London: McGraw-Hill.

Illich, I. 1999. *Deschooling society.* New York: Marion Boyars.

Inglis, S. 1994. *Making the most of action learning.* Brookfield, Vt.: Gower.

Ingram, H., K. Biermann, J. Cannon, J. Neil, and C. Waddle. 2000. Internalizing action learning: A company perspective—establishing critical success factors for action learning courses. *International Journal of Contemporary Hospitability Management* 12, no. 2: 107–113.

Isaacs, W. 1993. Taking flight: Dialogue, collective thinking, and organizational learning. *Organizational Dynamics* 22, no. 2: 24–39.

Johnson, D., and R. Johnson. 1989. *Cooperation and competition: Theory and research.* Edina, Minn.: Interaction Book Company.

Johnson, S., and K. Blanchard. 1998. *Who moved my cheese?* New York: Putnam.

Jones, M. 1990. Action learning as a new idea. *Journal of Management Development* 9, no. 5: 29–34.

Jubilerer, J. 1991. Action learning for competitive advantage. *Financier* 15, no. 9: 16–19.

Kable, J. 1989. Management development through action learning. *Journal of Management Development* 8, no. 2: 77–80.

Keene, A. 2000. Complexity theory: The changing role of leadership. *Industrial and Commercial Training* 32, no. 1: 15–18.

Keys, L. 1994. Action learning: Executive development of choice for the 1990s. *Journal of Management Development* 12, no. 8: 50–56.

Knowles, M., E. Holton, and R. Swanson. 1998. *The adult learner.* Houston: Gulf Publishing.

Kolb, D. 1984. *Experiential learning: Experience as the source of learning and development.* Englewood Cliffs, N.J.: Prentice-Hall.

Koo, L. 1999. Learning action learning. *Journal of Workplace Learning* 11, no. 3: 89–34.

Kotter, J. 1998. 21st century leadership. *Executive Excellence* 15, no. 5: 5–6.

Kouzes, J., and B. Posner. 2002. *The leadership challenge.* San Francisco: Jossey-Bass.

Lanahan, E. E., and L. Maldanado. 1998. Accelerated decision-making via action learning at the Federal Deposit Insurance Agency. *Performance Improvement Quarterly* 11, no. 1: 74–85.

Lawlor, A. 1997. The components of action learning. In M. Pedler, ed., *Action learning in practice,* 3rd ed., Aldershot, England: Gower.

Lawlor, A., and G. Boulden. 1982. *The application of action learning: A practical guide.* Geneva: International Labor Organization.

Lenderman, H., F. Lastar, and R. Lenderman. 2003. *Performance-based degrees earned at work: The Sodexho University story.* Prestonpan, U.K.: Prestoungrange University Press.

Lewis, A., and W. Marsh. 1997. Action learning: The development of field managers in the Prudential Insurance Company. *Journal of Management Development* 6, no. 2: 45–56.

Limerick, D., R. Passfield, and B. Cunnington. 1994. Transformational change: Towards an action learning organization. *The Learning Organization* 1, no. 2: 29–40.

MacNamara, M., M. Meyer, and A. Arnold. 1990. Management education and the challenge of action learning. *Higher Education* 19, no. 4: 419–433.

MacNamara, M., and W. H. Weeks. 1982. The action learning model of experiential learning for developing managers. *Human Relations* 35, no. 10: 879–901.

Margerison, C. 1988. Action learning and excellence in management development. *Journal of Management Studies* 32, no. 5: 43–53.

Marquardt, M. J. 1993. *Global human resource development.* Englewood Cliffs, N.J.: Prentice-Hall.

Marquardt, M. J. 1994. *The global learning organization.* New York: Irwin Professional Publishing.

Marquardt, M. J. 1996. Action learning: The cornerstone of building a learning organization. *Training and Development in Australia* 23, no. 4: 7–12.

Marquardt, M. J. 1997a. *Action learning.* Alexandria, Va.: ASTD Press.

Marquardt, M. J. 1997b. Action learning: An essential tool for corporate success. *HRD Focus,* 6–8.

Marquardt, M. J. 1997c. Action learning in the classroom. *Performance in Practice* (Summer): 4–5.

Marquardt, M. J. 1998. Using action learning with multicultural groups. *Performance Improvement Quarterly* 11, no. 1: 113–128.

Marquardt, M. J. 1999a. Action Learning. In *The resource guide to performance interventions.* San Francisco: Jossey-Bass.

Marquardt, M. J. 1999b. *Action learning in action.* Mountain View, Calif.: Davies-Black.

Marquardt, M. J. 1999c. Action learning: The cornerstone for building a learning organization. *Sozialpsychologie und Gruppendynamik* 24, no. 2: 3–16.

Marquardt, M. J. 2000. Action learning and leadership. *The Learning Organization* 7, no. 5: 233–240.

Marquardt, M. J. 2001a. Action learning: Does it work differently in different cultures? In S. Shankar, ed., *Action learning and action research for practitioners: An Asia-Pacific paradigm.* Sydney: Southern Cross University Press.

Marquardt, M. J. 2001b. Action learning. In S. Thiagarjan and E. Sanders, eds., *Performance Intervention Maps.* Alexandria, Va.: ASTD Press.

Marquardt, M. J. 2002. *Building the learning organization.* New York: McGraw-Hill.

Marquardt, M. J., and N. Berger. 2000. *Global leaders for the 21st century.* Albany, N.Y.: SUNY Press.

Marquardt, M. J., and T. Carter. 1998. Action learning and research at George Washington University. *Performance Improvement Quarterly* 11, no. 2: 59–71.

Marquardt, M. J., and L. Horvath. 2001. *Global teams.* Mountain View, Calif.: Davies-Black Publishing.

Marquardt, M. J., and D. Waddill. 2003. The power of learning in action learning: A conceptual analysis of how the five schools of adult learning theories are incorporated within the practice of action learning. *Proceedings of AHRD Conference,* Minneapolis.

Marsh, P., and B. Wood. 2001. Pressed for results: An action learning project in practice. *Industrial and Commercial Training* 33, no. 1: 32–36.

Marsick, V. 1988. Learning in the workplace: The case for critical reflectivity. *Adult Education Quarterly* 38, no. 4: 187–198.

Marsick, V. 1991. Action learning and reflection in the workplace. In J. Mezirow, ed., *Fostering critical reflection in adulthood.* San Francisco: Jossey-Bass.

Marsick, V. 1992. Experiential-based executive learning outside the classroom. *Journal of Management Development* 9, no. 5: 50–60.

Marsick, V., L. Cederholm, E. Turner, and T. Pearson. 1992. Action-reflection learning. *Training and Development* 46, no. 8: 63–66.

Marsick, V., and J. O'Neil. 1999. The many faces of action learning. *Management Learning* 30, no. 2: 159–176.

Mathews, K. M., M. White, and R. Long. 1999. Why study the complexity sciences in the social sciences? *Human Relations* 52, no. 4: 439–462.

McGill, I., and L. Beaty. 1995. *Action learning: A practitioner's guide,* 2nd ed. London: Kogan Page.

McLagan, P. 2003. The change-capable organization. *T + D* 57, no. 1: 50–58.

McLaughlin, H., and R. Thorp. 1993. Action learning: A paradigm in emergence. *British Journal of Management* 4, no. 1: 1003.

McNamara, C. 2002. *Authenticity circles facilitator's guide.* Minneapolis: Authenticity Consulting.

McNulty, N., and G. R. Canty. 1995. Proof of the pudding. *Journal of Management Development* 14, no. 1: 53–66.

Merriam, S. B., and R. S. Caffarella. 1999. *Learning in adulthood,* 3rd ed. San Francisco: Jossey-Bass.

Meyer, S. 2000. Action learning as a vehicle for organizational change culture. *Proceedings of Academy of Human Resources Development,* 594–599.

Mezirow, J. 1991. *Transformative dimensions of adult learning.* San Francisco: Jossey-Bass.

Moravic, M., and K. Wheeler. 1995. Mission possible. *Human Resource Executive* (special report), n.p.

Morris, J. 1991. Minding our Ps and Qs. In M. Pedler, ed., *Action learning in practice.* Aldershot, England: Gower.

Mumford, A. 1991. Learning in action. *Personnel Management* (July): 34–37.

Mumford, A. 1995. Developing others through action learning. *Industrial and Commercial Training* 27, no. 2: 19–27.

Mumford, A., ed. 1984. *Insights into action learning.* Bradford, England: MCB University Press.

Noel, J., and R. Charan. 1988. Leadership development at GE's Crotonville. *Human Resource Management* 27, no. 4: 433–447.

Noel, J., and R. Charan. 1992. GE brings global thinking to light. *Training and Development* 46, no. 7: 29–33.

Noel, J., and R. Dolitch. 1998. *Action learning.* San Francisco: Jossey-Bass.

Nonaka, I. 1994 . A dynamic theory of organizational knowledge creation. *Organization Science* 5, no. 1: 14–37.

Olson, E., and G. Eoyang. 2001. *Facilitating organizational change.* San Francisco: Jossey-Bass.

O'Neil, J. 1997. Set advising: More than just process. In M. Pedler, ed., *Action learning in practice,* 3rd ed. Aldershot, England: Gower.

Ormond, J. 1999. *Human learning.* Upper Saddle River, N.J.: Prentice-Hall.

Orr, J. E. 1990. Sharing knowledge, celebrating identity: Community memory in a service culture. In D. Middleton and D. Edwards, eds., *Collective remembering.* Newbury Park, Calif.: Sage.

Patrickson, M. 1998. Action learning. In F. Sofo, ed., *Human resource development: Paradigm, role, and practice choices.* Melbourne: Woodslane.

Pedler, M. 1996. *Action learning for managers.* London: Lemos & Crane.

Pedler, M. 1997. *Action learning in practice,* 3rd ed. Aldershot, England: Gower.

Pfeffer, J., and C. Fong. 2002. The end of business schools? Less success than meets the eye. *Academy of Management Learning and Education* 1, no. 1: 78–95.

Putnam, R. 2000. *Bowling alone.* New York: Simon & Schuster.

Raelin, J. A. 1997. Action learning and action science: Are they different? *Organizational Dynamics* (Summer): 21–33.

Raelin, J. A., and L. Michele. 1993. Learning by doing. *HR Magazine* 38, no. 2: 61–70.

Revans, R. W. 1965. *Science and management.* London: Macdonald.

Revans, R. W. 1971. *Developing effective managers: A new approach to business education.* London: Longmans.

Revans, R. W. 1980. *Action learning: New techniques for management.* London: Blond & Briggs.

Revans, R. W. 1981. Management, productivity, and risk: The way ahead. *Omega* 9, no. 2: 127–137.

Revans, R. W. 1982a. *The origins and growth of action learning.* Bromley, England: Chartwell-Bratt.

Revans, R. W. 1982b. What is action learning? *Journal of Management Development* 1, no. 3: 64–75.

Revans, R. W. 1983. *ABC of action learning.* Bromley, England: Chartwell-Bratt.

Revans, R. W. 1986. Action learning in a developing country. *Management Decision* 24, no. 6: 3–7.

Rogers, C. 1994. *Freedom to learn.* New York: Macmillan.

Rotter, J. B. 1954. *Social learning and clinical psychology.* Englewood Cliffs, N.J.: Prentice-Hall.

Sandelands, E. 1998. Creating an online library to support a virtual learning community. *Internet Research* 8, no. 1: 75–84.

Sashkin, M., and M. Sashkin. 2003. *Leadership that.* San Francisco: Berrett-Koehler.

Schein, E. 1997. *Organizational culture and leadership.* San Francisco: Jossey-Bass.

Schön, D. 1983. *The reflective practitioner: How professionals think in action.* New York: Basic Books.

Schuman, S. 1996. The role of facilitation in collaborative groups. In C. Huxham, ed., *The search for collaborative advantage.* London: Sage.

Senge, P. 1990. *The fifth discipline.* New York: Doubleday.

Skinner, B. F. 1971. *Beyond freedom and dignity.* New York: Knopf.

Smith, D. 1992. Company based projects: Using action learning to develop consultancy skills. *Journal of Management Development* 11, no. 1: 12–24.

Smith, P. 2001. Action learning and reflective practice in project environments that are related to leadership development. *Management Learning* 32, no. 1: 31–48.

Sundstrom, E., et al. 1999. *Supporting work team effectiveness.* San Francisco: Jossey-Bass.

Sutton, D. 1991. A range of applications. In M. Pedler, ed., *Action learning in practice,* 2nd ed. Aldershot, England: Gower.

Sveiby, K. 1997. *The new organizational wealth: Managing and measuring knowledge-based assets.* San Francisco: Berrett-Koehler.

Thorndike, E. L., E. O. Bregman, J. W. Tilton, and E. Woodyard. 1928. *Adult learning.* New York: Macmillan.

Trompenaars, F. 1994. *Riding the waves of culture.* New York: McGraw-Hill.

Tversky, A., and D. Kahneman. 1974. Judgment under uncertainty: Heuristics and biases. *Science* 18, no. 185: 1124–1131.

Vaill, P. 1996. *Learning as a way of being.* San Francisco: Jossey-Bass.

Vince, R., and L. Martin. 1993. Inside action learning: An exploration of the psychology and politics of the action learning model. *Management Education and Development* 24, no. 3: 205–215.

Weick, K. 1995. *Sensemaking in organizations.* Thousand Oaks, Calif.: Sage.

Weinstein, K. 1995. *Action learning: A journey in discovery and development.* London: HarperCollins.

Wenger, E., R. McDermott, and W. Snyder. 2002. *Cultivating communities of practice.* Cambridge: Harvard Business School Press.

Wheatley. M. J. 1992. *Leadership and the new science.* San Francisco: Berrett-Koehler.

Yoong, P., and B. Gallupe. 2001. Action learning and groupware technologies: A case study in GSS facilitation research. *Information Technology & People* 14, no. 1: 78–88.

York, L., J. O'Neil, and V. Marsick, eds. 1999. *Action learning: Successful strategies for individual, team, and organizational development.* San Francisco: Berrett-Koehler.

Zuber-Skerritt, O. 1995. Developing a learning organization through management education by action learning. *Learning Organization* 2, no. 2: 36–54.

Zuboff, S. 1988. *In the age of the smart machine: The future of work and power.* New York: Basic Books.

Index

absenteeism, 185

action(s): description of, 89; development of, 12, 22; group member's power to implement, 46; as learning opportunities, 101; power of, 105–106; recommending of, 189–190; reflecting on, 102–103; strategies. See strategies; taking of, 12, 102–103, 107, 189; time frame for, 93

action learning: benefits of, 192–195; breadth of, 131; climate of, 136; coach. See action learning coach; competencies developed in. See competencies; components of, 2–4; confidentiality of, 182–183; definition of, 2; demonstration of, 166–167; depth of, 131; description of, 1; disciplines involved in, 10–11; framework of, 102, 104–105; ground rules for. See ground rules; history of, 1; implementation steps for. See implementation steps; intensity of, 130–131; knowledge obtained by, 110; leadership development by, 17, 120–121, 194–195; leadership training vs., 17, 120–121; learning achieved in, 109–110, 114–115, 126–128, 131; management's support for, 161–164, 192; open-group, 6; organizations that have used, 106; power of, 130–131, 195; premise of, 27, 102; problem-solving approach of, 21–23, 69–70, 194; proponent of, 164; reasons for success of, 10–11; single-problem, 35–36; speed of, 131; stages of, 12–13; structure in, 7; success with, 10–11, 23; variations of, 4

action learning champion, 55, 182

action learning coach: action learning group member's role as, 53; adminis-trator role of, 153; attitude of, 152, 156; attributes of, 154–156; authenticity of, 154; body language of, 150; characteristics of, 155; checklist for, 158, 175; co-coaching by, 174–175; commitment to learning of, 156; confidence of, 155; courage of, 154; description of, 4, 22, 133–134; empowering by, 141–142; experience as group member of, 174; external, 173; facilitator's role as, 139–141; focus of, 53; impact of, 156; importance of, 134–135; internal, 173–175; interventions by, 141–147, 154–155; learning climate facilitated by, 136; listening skills of, 156; motivation by, 141–142; multiple-problem action learning group role of, 37; neutrality of, 137; objectivity of, 138; permanent, 135–136; person who serves as, 135–136; planning skills of, 155; power to intervene by, 9–10, 137–139; preparing of, 174–175; problem reframing role of, 97; problem solving by, 138–139; questions by, 133–134, 136–137, 142–151, 154; responsibilities of, 9, 53, 136; roles of, 97, 133, 152–154, 180–181; rotating of, 135–136, 173–174; self-awareness of, 156; self-confidence of, 156; skills of, 154–156; statements by, 137; style of, 180–181; trainer/teacher role of, 153; trust of, 155; values of, 152, 155; workshop participation by, 166–167

action learning group: accountability of, 49; authority of, 31; champion of, 182; characteristics of, 18–19, 45, 62–66; checklist for, 67, 183; cohesiveness of, 54, 56, 66, 73–74;

action learning group, *cont'd*
commitment to solving problem, 62;
common purpose of, 63; composition
common purpose of, 63; composition
of, 45; concrete experience of, 114;
cooperative, 61–62; criteria for inclu-
sion in, 176; definition of, 3; dialogue
in, 82–85; diversity of, 47, 51; environment of, 75, 111–112; expectations of, 49; formation of, 12; full-
time, 94, 179; highly effective, 62–66;
intactness of, 56; learning in, 18–19;
life stages of, 64; meeting of. *See*
meeting; sessions; membership in, 5,
21; members of. *See* action learning
group members; multiple-problem,
5–6, 35; and mutual respect, 66;
norms of, 64–65; outsider participation in, 56; part-time, 94; personalities involved in, 57–58; and problem
familiarity, 30; reasoning strategies
of, 62; sessions with. *See* meetings;
sessions; silence in, 150; single-problem, 5–6, 35; size of, 21, 48–49, 176;
sponsor of, 181; strategy development by, 104; subject-matter experts
in, 59; trust in, 66; virtual, 60–61;
willingness to work with others,
63–64
action learning group members: absenteeism by, 185; action taking by,
89–90; anecdotal communication by,
99, 101; appointing of, 56, 176–177;
attendance by, 47–48, 54, 171;
checklist for, 178; coach role of, 53;
commitment of, 46, 52–53, 62; communication by, 48; conflicts among,
185; consensus by, 48, 54, 63, 97;
courage of, 64; diversity of, 47; domination by, 184–185; enthusiasm of,
54; external, 177; familiarity with
problem by, 47; implementation
power of, 46; knowledge of, 46;
learning by, 66, 110–111; learning
skills of, 124– 125; outsiders' inclu-
sion as, 56, 177; participation by, 48;
personalities of, 57–58; problem presenter role of, 51–53; problem sponsor role of, 55; question asking by,
54, 64, 76, 80–81; respect by, 66;
responsibility of, 53–54; roles of,
51–55; selection of, 45–48, 176;
support of, 66; volunteers as, 55–56,
176–177
action learning program: analyzing of,
191–192; types of, 6

action plan, 99
adaptive problems, 32
administrator role, 153
affective questions, 77
analytical questions, 78
analytic/rationalistic approach to problem solving, 90–91
anchoring, 41
anecdotal communication, 99, 101
anthropology, 11
appreciative inquiry, 11, 150
attitude, 130–131, 156

behavioral learning, 129
biology, 11
"breakthrough learning," 20

capability, 104
career advancement, 20
chaos, 7–8
chaos theory, 11, 91
checklists: action learning group, 67,
183, 196; action learning group
members, 178; coach, 158, 175;
finalizing of activities, 193; implementation of actions, 191; learning,
132; management support for action
learning, 163; pilot testing, 190;
problem, 43, 172; questions, 87; recommending of actions, 190; reflection, 87; reflective inquiry, 87;
reframing of problem, 188; sessions,
186; strategy development, 188;
workshop, 168
clarifying questions, 78
closed questions, 78
coach. *See* action learning coach
co-coaching, 174–175
cognitive learning, 128–129
cohesiveness, 54, 56, 66, 73–74,
123–124
commitment: of action learning group
members, 46, 52–53, 62; by coach,
156; to learning, 4; management support for action learning, 192; to problem solving, 122
communication: description of, 48; dialogue. *See* dialogue
competencies: description of, 116; individual development, 116–118; leadership learning, 118–120; professional
development, 116–118
conceptualizing, 114–115
concrete experience, 114
confidentiality, 135, 182–183
conflicts, 185

constructivist learning, 130
cooperative work groups, 61–62
crisis, 42
critical reflection skills, 20

debate, 83
development: individual, 116–118, 195; professional, 19–20, 116–118
dialogue: action learning role of, 84; benefits of, 83–84; characteristics of, 82–83; debate vs., 83; definition of, 82; discussion vs., 83; stages of creating, 82–85
discipline, 130–131
discussion, 83
diversity: of action learning group, 47, 51; importance of, 59

edge of chaos, 7
education, 10
emotional intelligence, 119
emotions, 119
empathy, 20, 119
empowerment, 117, 135, 141–142
environment, 75, 111–112
ethics, 11
explicit knowledge, 115–116
explorative questions, 78

facilitator, 139–141
focus, 104
framing of goals, 97–98
fresh questions, 78
full-time action learning group, 94, 179

generalizing, 114–115
goals: action learning group's focus on, 63; agreement on, 122–123; determining of, 12; formulating of, 97–98, 107; framing of, 97–98; setting of, 180
ground rules: benefits of, 9–10; coach's power to intervene, 9–10, 137–138; statements only in response to questions, 8–9, 21–22, 75–76, 96
group: action learning. *See* action learning group; dynamics of, 10; problem-solving, 21
group-created knowledge, 116
growth: problem as opportunity for, 42; professional, 19–20

humanist learning, 129–130

implementation steps: action learning group members. *See* action learning

group members; action learning group orientation and preparation, 177–183; coach selection and preparation, 173–175. *See also* action learning coach; finalizing of activities, 191–192; implementing of strategies, 189–191; management support, 161–164, 192; preparatory workshop. *See* preparatory workshop; problem or project selection, 169–173; sessions. *See* sessions
individual development, 116–118, 195
inquiry skills, 20
integrative approach to problem solving, 90–91
intensity, 130–131
internal action learning model, 113
interventions: coach's role in, 9–10, 141–147, 154–155; power for implementing, 9–10, 137–139; timing of, 154–155

knowledge: acquiring of, 126; action learning effects on, 109–110, 115–116; capture of, 14–15; concrete experience for, 114; creating of, 126; definition of, 118; explicit, 115–116; generalizing and conceptualizing, 114–115; group-created, 116; group member, 46; observing and reflecting, 114; programmed, 101, 116, 121; quality of, 90; questions' effect on, 77; self-knowledge, 117; storing of, 126; tacit, 115–116; transfer of, 14–15; transferring of, 126; types of, 115–116
Kolb learning model, 113

leaders: competency development by, 118–120; mental models, 120–121; support for action learning by, 161–164
leadership: need for, 14; skills, 119
leadership development: action learning for, 17, 120–121, 194–195; of competencies, 118–120; programs for, 16–17, 120–121; questions' role in, 74
leading questions, 78
learning: action learning generation of, 109–110, 114–115, 126–128, 131; action learning group member's responsibility, 66, 110–111; application of, 118; behavioral, 129; "breakthrough," 20; capturing of, 111–112; case study-based approach to, 17;

learning, *cont'd*
checklist for, 132; climate of, 136;
coaching effects on, 151–152;
cognitive, 128–129; commitment to,
4; constructivist, 130; creating of,
111–112; cycles of, 113–115; developing of, 111–112; humanist,
129–130; importance of, 22; individual, 195; internal action model of,
113; Kolb model of, 113; long-term
capabilities, 111; need for, 15; opportunities for, 90, 112; organizational,
124–126; participant, 19–20; principles of, 126–128; problem as moti-
vator for, 30–31; questions' role in,
74–75; social, 129; stages of,
114–115; team-based, 121–124;
theories of, 128–130; time for, 163;
willingness for, 66, 123
learning organizations: action learning
and, 124, 194; competitive advantages of, 194; components of, 124;
creation of, 18–19, 124; subsystems
of, 18; transformation of, 125
learning skills, 125
life science, 11
limitations, 121
linear thinking, 91–92
listening: coach's skills, 156; questions
and, 73–74; reflective, 3

management science, 10
management support for action learning,
161–164, 192
meetings: arranging of, 178–179; confir-
mation of, 179; domination of,
184–185; duration of, 180, 183; frequency of, 179–180; questions asked
during, 142–147. *See also* sessions
mental models, 120
motivation, 141–142
multiple-problem action learning: advantages of, 37–38; description of, 36,
169; elements of, 36–37
multiple-problem action learning groups:
advantages of, 37–38; coach's role in,
37; description of, 5–6, 35; meeting
of, 37; members from different organizations, 38; questions in, 146
multiple questions, 78

Newtonian physics, 92
norms: action learning group, 64–65;
description of, 7–8, 123; statements
only in response to questions, 8–9,
21–22, 75–76, 96

open-group action learning, 6
open questions, 77
open systems and engineering, 11
order, 7–8
organization(s): action learning benefits
for, 192–195; challenges for, 14–15;
leadership of, 14, 119; learning. *See*
learning organizations; single-problem action learning benefits for, 35;
transformation to learning organization, 194
organizational learning, 124–126

part-time action learning group, 94
pilot test, 115, 187, 189–190
political science, 11
preconceptions, 41
preparatory workshop: arranging of,
164–165; benefits of, 168–169;
checklist for, 168; coach's participation in, 166–167; content of,
165–168; description of, 164; logistics for, 165; opportunity to attend,
165; questions asking during, 167–168
presenting of problem: action learning
group member's responsibility,
51–53; areas presented, 171–172;
biases in, 41–42; in multiple-problem
groups, 39; preparing for, 39–40;
questions after, 40, 80; "real" problem identified after, 40–41, 96; in
single-problem groups, 38–39
probing questions, 78
problem(s): action taken on, 3–4; adaptive, 32; characteristics of, 3, 21;
checklist for, 43, 172; definition of, 3;
description of, 27; examples of,
33–34; familiarity with, 30; feasibility
of, 29–31; group members' familiarity with, 47; growth opportunities
associated with, 42; importance of,
28–29; learning opportunities gained
from, 30–31, 138–139; multiple, 169;
no existing solution for, 29; opportunities associated with, 42; presentation of, 12. *See also* problem presenter; presenting of. *See* presenting of
problem; purpose of, 27; "real,"
40–41, 96; reframing of, 12, 97, 107,
186–188; selection of, 28–29,
169–173; significance of, 30, 52; single, 35–36, 169; synonyms for, 28;
technical, 32; time frame for resolving, 172; types of, 31–33, 170; understanding of, 71, 95–97; urgency of,
29, 52, 134, 137–138

problem presenter: action learning group member's role as, 51–53; aspects of problem presented by, 171–172; authority of, 172–173; question asking by, 80–81; selection of, 170–171; withholding of information by, 185–186

problem solving: action learning approach to, 21–23, 69–70, 194; analytic/rationalistic approach to, 90–91; benefits of, 109; coach's role in, 138; commitment to, 122; development of, 15–16; integrative approach to, 90–91; questions for, 73; reflective inquiry for, 93; systems and tools for, 105; systems thinking in, 91–93

problem-solving stages: goal framing and formulating, 97–98; overview of, 95; strategy development and testing, 98–102; taking of action, 102–103; time distribution in, 103–104; understanding and reframing the problem, 95–97

problem sponsor, 51, 55

professional growth and development, 19–20, 116–118

programmed knowledge, 101, 116, 121

psychology, 10

quantum physics, 92

question(s): action learning group sessions, 142–147; affective, 77; analytical, 78; appreciative inquiry for phrasing of, 150; artistic nature of, 85–86; asking of, 54, 78, 80–81, 149–150; benefits of, 72–75; characteristics of, 79–80; checklist for, 87; clarifying, 78; closed, 78; coach's responsibility to ask, 133–134, 136–137, 142–151, 154; cohesive benefits of, 73–74; connection-creating, 78; courage to ask, 64, 123; cultural considerations, 85; description of, 3; explorative, 78; follow-up, 148–149; fresh, 78; "good," 79–80; importance of, 71–72; knowledge enhancement and advancement by, 77; leadership development benefits of, 74; leading, 78; learning enhancement benefits of, 74–75; multiple, 78; open, 77; persons who ask, 80–81; poetic nature of, 85–86; power of, 71–72, 151; after presenting of problem, 40, 52; probing, 78; problem-solving benefits of, 73; problem understood through, 96; purposes of,

69; reflection on, 81; reflective, 78; response to, 52, 73; results of, 79; statements made in response to, 8–9, 21–22, 75–76, 96; team-building benefits of, 73–74; types of, 77–78, 143–144

questioning: abilities for, 20; learning obtained through, 112

reflection: checklist for, 87; description of, 81; elements of, 81–82; self-critical, 112; time allotted for, 138

reflective inquiry: benefits of, 81; checklist for, 87; description of, 51, 58, 70, 74–75; elements of, 81; limitations explored through, 121; problem solving using, 93

reflective listening, 3

reflective questions, 78

reframing of problem, 97, 107, 186–188

representativeness, 41

respect, 66, 123

Revans, Reg, 1, 33, 49, 98, 102

self-awareness, 119, 156

self-confidence, 156

self-critical reflection, 112

self-knowledge, 117

self-learning, 117–118

sessions: arranging of, 178–179; checklist for, 186; conflicts in, 185; domination of, 184–185; duration of, 183; frequency of, 184; goal setting, 180; learning purposes of, 180; pitfalls experienced in, 184–186; questions asked during, 142–147; scheduling of, 181–182; time between, 184; withholding of information in, 185–186. *See also* meetings

silence, 150

single-problem action learning: benefits of, 35–36; description of, 169; groups involved in, 5–6, 35–36; presenting of problem, 38–39

skills, 117–118

social learning, 129

sociology, 10

sponsor: group, 181; problem, 51, 55

statements only in response to questions, 8–9, 21–22, 75–76, 96

storming, 65

strategies: development of, 98–101, 107, 123, 186–188; implementation of, 189–191; testing of, 101–102. *See also* action(s)

structure, 7

subject-matter experts, 59
success: of action learning, 10–11, 23; problem as opportunity for, 42
system alpha, 105, 187
system beta, 105, 187
system gamma, 105, 187
systems thinking, 20, 91–93, 96

tacit knowledge, 115–116
team(s): growth of, 121; learning in, 121–124; need for, 14; traits of, 122–123
team building: action learning for, 195; description of, 17–18; questions' role in, 73–74

technical problems, 32
time frame: for action learning stages, 103–104; for action taking, 93; for problem resolution, 172
trainer/teacher role, 153
trust, 66, 123–124, 155

virtual action learning group, 60–61
vulnerability, 52

will, 104
workshop. *See* preparatory workshop